DATA AND TEACHING

Published by Teachers College Press, 1234 Amsterdam Avenue, New York, NY 10027

Copyright © 2018 by Teachers College, Columbia University

Cover photos: Rabbit by Eric Isselee via Shutterstock; chalkboard by Open Grid Scheduler via Flickr, under a creative commons attribution license; light effect by Flavio Takemoto via sxc.hu, under a creative commons attribution license.

The research reported in this book was supported by a grant from the Spencer Foundation.

Library of Congress Cataloging-in-Publication Data is available at loc.gov

ISBN 978-0-8077-5907-3 (paper)
ISBN 978-0-8077-5908-0 (hardcover)
ISBN 978-0-8077-7634-6 (ebook)

Printed on acid-free paper
Manufactured in the United States of America

25 24 23 22 21 20 19 18   8 7 6 5 4 3 2 1

The coauthors dedicate this book to
Beth and Harry;
Stuart and Adrienne;
and Robert, Michelle, and Mark.

Contents

Preface

Data use has recently transformed whole fields of contemporary life, and some people expect that teaching might be next. They especially include policymakers and policy drivers—from governors and superintendents to technology entrepreneurs and curriculum marketers. They hope that data and data use in teaching can help schools impacted by poverty beat the odds their students face in learning. We share this hope to a great extent, though we are also cautious about magical thinking. And in the research we report in this book, we encountered a significant amount of magical thinking with regard to data use in teaching. It seemed to us to be the product of a tendency to think of teaching itself as a simpler thing than it actually is, and a tendency to think of innovation in practice as easier to achieve than it typically proves to be. We argue in this book that teaching is in fact very complex, and that innovation aiming to change it must pass through multiple levels of conceptual, contextual, and practical challenges. These require nimble negotiation and problem-solving, plus a willingness to engage in and accommodate adaptive redesign.

Of course, we do not just *argue* these points. We also illustrate them richly, and we advise our readers on how to deal with them. The book follows the innovation we call *data use in teaching* from its origins in broadly popular sense-making, through policy adoption, commercial exploitation, local adaptation, and on to its ultimate target: the practices of schooling and teaching in particular schools. Our depiction is grounded in research we conducted within tough and ambitious contexts. These are nine schools in New York City (five of them elementary, and four of them middle)—all among the city's most poverty impacted, though also among the most active in attempting to use data to support their teaching. Between 2012 and 2015, we studied these schools and their data use empathetically, but also tough mindedly, and this book is the outcome. What we sometimes found was chaotic implementation, and we portray the chaos plainly—especially in two of the four chapters that we characterize as *deep dives* (or up-close and intensive portraits of data use in action within a particular school). However, we also found imaginative and productive implementation—the kind that can boost learning, and we portray this plainly too—especially in the two other deep dive chapters. Of course, we conceal the identity of these schools by changing names, locations, and other factors.

This book is one product of an effort by the Spencer Foundation to help solve an important problem in U.S. educational policymaking. Here is how the foundation described this problem in a 2012 Request for Proposals (RFP):

> Current educational policy reforms emphasize data-based decisionmaking in the absence of a strong body of research showing whether, when, and how data of particular kinds can be used to produce improved learning and performance. The emphasis on collecting and providing data seems often to be rooted in a belief that educators who are presented information under data-driven improvement schemes will know how to make sense of it and change their practice (Spencer Foundation, 2012, p. 1).

The RFP emphasized data use by teachers of grades K–8, and called for research that "not only shows whether, when, and how data should be used, but also describes the contexts and conditions in which data use actually takes place" (p.1).

The lead author of this book, Joseph McDonald, responded to the Spencer RFP on behalf of the Research Alliance for New York City Schools (RANYCS)—an organization committed to rigorous research that matters to New York schools, and that advances equity and school quality. His collaborators in preparing what proved to be a successful proposal, and in designing the research, were NYU Professor James Kemple, executive director of RANYCS, and NYU Professor Susan Neuman. The book's second and third authors, Nora Isacoff and Dana Karin, joined the research team at the beginning of the data collection phase. Under this RFP, the foundation funded other research efforts—working in multiple contexts across the U.S.—and it brought all the teams together frequently over the course of the next 3 years, to discuss their methods and findings with each other. We acknowledge these extraordinary colleagues below. Meanwhile, to support the teams and also guide their work, the Spencer Foundation also launched a major literature review of data use in schooling. This review was published in 2012, in full volumes of both the *American Journal of Education* (volume 118, number 2), and *Teachers College Record* (volume 114, number 11). The review shaped our data collection, and also this book. For those readers interested in the details of how we conducted our research, we refer you to the Appendix.

We start this book with some basics in Part I. First is an overview of the kinds of data we focused on in our study and why (Chapter 1). Next is an exploration of what teaching really is, and why it resists simplistic innovation (Chapter 2). Finally, we take up the matter of what data use in teaching is, including where it came from, and what it involves beyond teachers and students (Chapter 3). We illustrate these three chapters with data from all nine of our schools. Then, in Part II, we take deep dives into two elementary and two middle schools selected from the nine schools we studied (Chapters 4 through 7). Between all the chapters, we present a series of briefs for educators on what we call *New Directions* for teaching and learning with data. We have based these not only on our own research and practice, but also on the research and practice of others we cite. We offer them as a means of evading magical thinking, and of fulfilling hopes for better schooling, richer teaching, and deeper learning. Finally, we conclude the book with a short distillation of our major findings and of the value and hope we see in them.

As a project of the Research Alliance for New York City Schools, our research was oriented from the start to be useful to practitioners, to serve as a reflecting tool for the schools that participated in the research, and ultimately to serve as a practice guide for other schools within and beyond New York City. What we call our *New Directions*—or practice-focused briefs— emerged from this orientation.

Acknowledgments

We thank the Research Alliance for New York City Schools for its encouragement and support in pursuing the research we report here. In particular, we appreciate director James Kemple's and deputy director Adriana Villavicencio's assistance in shaping the study and the sample of schools, and Adwoa Adjei-Gyampo's and Nina Siman's efforts in providing ongoing support. Thanks also to Tom Gold's foundational research at RANYCS on an early New York City data management system called ARIS. In this same category of contributors to and great supporters of our research, we also thank our colleague Susan Neuman, who first proposed the study, helped in fashioning the research design, and contributed substantially to data collection and analysis. We lost her eventually to another important project, but she made a mark on this one. Other colleagues who helped significantly are professors Rosa Pietanza and Carolyn Strom. The first was our thought partner in site selection as well as our guide through the thicket of terminologies and materials that make up data use in teaching in New York City schooling. And the second conducted early research in several schools.

We also thank our Spencer project colleagues. They include the leaders of other teams like ours, studying data use in teaching in other places; scholars who visited the 3-year seminar that the Foundation hosted; and Foundation staff who facilitated the seminar so skillfully. In alphabetical order, they are Michael Barber, Nicole Barnes, Hilda Borko, Melissa Braaten, Christopher Bradford, Catherine Brighton, Andrea Bueschel, Joan Buttram, Amanda Datnow, John Easton, Caroline Ebby, Elizabeth Farley-Ripple, Helenrose Fives, Maricelle Garcia, Brette Garner, Jennifer Greene, Ilana Horn, Matt Kloser, Tammy Kolbe, Tonya Moon, Pavithra Nagarajan, Vicki Park, Carolyn Riehl, Tom Schwandt, Jim Spillane, Jon Supovitz, Joan Talbert, and Brenda Turnbull.

Three other scholars also had a pronounced impact on our research and on this book—though from a distance, and by means of their mentoring of the lead researcher and writer, followed by his next-generation mentoring of his coauthors. Donald A. Schön provided a conceptual framework that guided the analysis of our findings. David K. Cohen provided another framework that guided our understanding of what teaching is. And Sara Lawrence-Lightfoot provided the inspiration and strategy for writing about complex phenomena richly and respectfully.

We are very grateful to our early readers who provided essential help in shaping the book. They include Carole Saltz, Peter Sclafani, Susan Liddicoat, and two perceptive peer reviewers. They also include Leslie Siskin and members of her monthly NYU salon on schooling and faithful and insightful readers Sherry King, Beth McDonald, Binh Thai, and Alan Dichter (as well as members of his network of CUNY-affiliated school leaders).

Finally, we acknowledge the contributions to our research and this book made by the educators who invited us into their practices. Although their identities are concealed herein by pseudonyms, their work, thinking, and energy are on full display on nearly every page.

PART I

THE BASICS OF
DATA USE AND TEACHING

CHAPTER 1

What Is Data?

The word *data* originated as the plural of the Latin word *datum*, but it is used now also as a singular noun, and we follow that convention in this book. At the most elemental or raw level, data consists of empirically discerned traces of some phenomenon of interest as captured by some device. In education, the device may be a voice recorder, clicker, notebook, camera, laptop, pop quiz, standardized test, teacher-created test, or notation by hand on a checklist or rubric. The use of the word *data* signifies that the traces of experience are to be taken as facts—not in some incontrovertible sense, but in the sense of legitimizing their usefulness for further thinking and action. As Bryk, Gomez, Grunow, and LeMahieu (2015) suggest, use of the word *data* also implicitly involves an embrace of variation—an acknowledgment that what teachers and schools pursue can only be achieved in terms of some distribution of outcomes. In our minds, the word is also associated with what is called *knowledge management*—learning to work smarter by sharing, discussing, and leveraging information (Brown & Duguid, 2000; Nonaka, 2007; Wenger, McDermott, & Snyder, 2002).

LEVELS OF DATA

Two levels of data are particularly relevant to schooling and teaching today. In this book, we use the terms *big-test data* and *intimate data* to refer to them. Note that in most parts of the book, we avoid the terms *formative* and *summative*, which are more associated with function than scale, and might prove confusing here. In this book, we continually zoom from big to intimate scale and vice versa. What we call *big-test data* is the kind that districts or charter management groups get back from states and standardized testing vendors, that they add to for purposes of reporting to state education departments and the federal government, and that they share with principals and increasing numbers of school-level data managers or "coaches." This data derives largely from federally mandated annual testing in literacy and math, and from other policy-mandated testing—for example, of English language learners (ELLs).

Intimate data is student performance data that practitioners collect themselves. Some of this is associated with what is often called formal classroom assessment—for example, teacher-created quizzes, tests, projects, or exit tickets (quick reports from students on what they learned from a particular episode of teaching). And some is associated with informal classroom assessment—by means, for example, of teacher observation and questioning, or post-teaching reflection. It is important to note that some intimate data is associated with *standardized* assessment. That is, it is collected and analyzed in formally specified ways, and often stored in online data management systems designed to analyze it. Still, teachers themselves collect it, and gain in the process an intimacy with what it reports. For example, a widely practiced form of standardized intimate data gathering in the schools we studied—both the elementary schools and the middle schools—involves *running records* or formal inventories by teachers of their students' oral reading skills and reading problems.

For the most part, we deal in this book with data at these two scales. Yet in using the term *big-test data*, we deliberately evoke the term *big data*—or what we call *genuinely big data*. This is the kind of data that comes in sets much too big for your laptop to process—in other words, a third scale of data. Examples of genuinely big data include data from the vast universe of digitized buying and selling, managed so as to predict, produce, and deliver shampoo (or something else) that you think you need; the billions of pixels from sophisticated cameras in NBA arenas, which are analyzed to discover best court positions for successful basketball shots; and, in education, the covertly captured user data from thousands of online learning programs that are analyzed in order to create new online programs or to improve existing ones. We have more to say about this third scale of data at the end of this chapter, though it is mostly speculative. In fact, the biggest data sets we saw in the schools we studied were merely compilations of big-test data and administrative data (for example, regarding attendance or ability/disability status). And as it turned out, school-level data managers actually did sometimes manage these data sets on their laptops.

Even if *big-test data* is not nearly as big as *big data*, the distinction between it and intimate data is important to make and to ponder. Big-test data plays a crucial role in U.S. schooling today, as does its intimate cousin. And the difference is palpable for people who work in schools. Calling attention to the difference is important, we think, for developing systems to support responsible data use at *both* scales. As it turns out, nearly everyone we interviewed or observed (both teachers and school administrators) regard both big-test data and intimate data as valuable. However, most also believe that school outsiders—whom our interviewees often referred to as "they" or "them"—do not appreciate the value to teaching of intimate data, particularly of the nonstandardized variety.

In coding our own data from this study, we distinguished between references (by any words) to big-test data, and references (by any words) to intimate data. Our initial analysis based on this coding suggested that our research participants were 2.25 times more likely to talk about intimate data than about big-test data. As we looked more closely at the coded segments of transcript, however, we discovered that a reference to one of these (no matter how many times uttered) was never very far from a reference to the other. We think this suggests that school-based educators today are living with—and often thinking about—the associations of and tensions between big-test data and intimate data. We think this is healthy, and we wish more policymakers were doing the same.

WHAT EDUCATORS TALK ABOUT WHEN THEY TALK ABOUT DATA

In order to discern patterns of meaning in school-based educators' talk about data, we drew on the 75 analytic memos of our research transcripts that we coded as *what's data* (see the Appendix for further details of our research coding). We found that the number one data category educators talk about (at 29% of the memos) is data about what students know or don't know in terms of knowledge and skills that teachers specifically and deliberately aimed to teach them. This is hardly surprising, given that both big-test assessment and intimate classroom assessment focus resolutely on this target. Obviously, teachers need to know whether or not their students learned what they taught. There is a problem, however, if this focus crowds out opportunities for teachers to learn other crucial things too. Happily, one of these other crucial things comes next at a respectable 21%: data about students' thinking processes. Of course, this finding does not mean that educators in our study actually devoted this much of their engagement with students to figuring out what students were thinking. In fact, in our observations of teaching, we found that teachers often passed up opportunities to ask (in the face of "a wrong answer" or a confusing one) something like "Can you say more about what you're thinking?" Still, the code count here at least suggests strong interest in the matter.

What comes next in our memo code count, however, is disappointing. Only 6% of data-related talk was about students' misconceptions. Teachers' interest in misconceptions is crucial not only to help students unlearn "wrong answers," but at a deeper level, to help them displace naive mental models with more sophisticated ones (National Research Council, 2001). And even less of the data-related talk—at 4 percent—was about students' metacognitive skills and inclinations, or students' understanding of their own thinking and learning. Yet metacognition, according to learning science, is a major path to deep learning (National Research Council, 2001).

Beyond number counts, we were, of course, also interested in *how* the educators we studied talked about data, and with what degrees of subtlety and acknowledgment of complexity. One common pattern was what we came to think of as hyperrational, or cut and dried. Here, for example, is a middle school principal responding to a question about how her school organizes for data use in teaching:

> Okay, so once we get the state results—the exams—our data specialist makes charts, so that every teacher is given a data folder, and that data folder includes the results on the exam, the item analysis [which students answered which questions correctly and not], how many of the kids in that teacher's classroom were ELLs, how many of the kids are SPED [eligible for special education services]. Then, in September, every teacher gives a diagnostic. In literacy, it's a writing piece, and a running record in reading [individualized read-aloud with miscue analysis]; and in math it's math skills; in social studies, it's an essay about historical events. Then the teachers take that information, and they enter it into a tracking system that we've devised. It looks like this [shows a printout of a complex Google Docs spreadsheet]. And then we design the curriculum.

By "hyperrational," we mean a system description that spells out data flow (as in charts, folders, and tracking systems), but glosses over interpretation (as in "then we design the curriculum"), or put another way, a focus on data collection but not data use. Such talk about data seems to suggest that data is an agent rather than information for an agent. It puts data, rather than teaching and learning, at the heart of *data use in teaching*.

VALIDITY AND EFFICIENCY IN DATA USE

The usefulness of data systems in all fields of practice depends on how well these systems ensure the validity of the data they process, and also on how efficiently they support the practices they are intended to serve—in this case, teaching and learning.

Validity

As a construct in assessment, validity has to do with the relationship of data to legitimate inference, and with the reliability of data systems over time in maintaining this relationship. We're talking about a kind of truthfulness here, where the word *truth* covers such questions as: what writing really is, what students' responses to a particular writing assessment really signify about them as writers, and whether the assessment captures this reliably across time and cases.

Teachers and school leaders need to consider validity continually—indeed, whenever they consider questions of what students now understand, and what they should learn next. But this requires three things that tend to be poorly distributed in U.S. schools. First, access to deep content knowledge—that is, content knowledge with strong disciplinary or interdisciplinary footing. This is needed to discern the value of particular big-test items to a larger domain, to create valid intimate assessment items, and even to devise and carry out valid teaching probes.

Second, many schools have poor collective understanding of standardized testing. In our research, for example, we found instances of schools basing decisions about what to teach in a given year on individual items from the previous year's big test. But the validity of a standardized test overall in accurately sampling some domain does *not* extend to individual test items. For example, knowledge of a particular word—say, the verb *articulate*—shouldn't be added to the 4th-grade curriculum this year just because it appeared on last year's 4th-grade English Language Arts (ELA) test. Some other word meant to discriminate among levels of 4th-graders' vocabulary will replace it next year.

Finally, many schools need to expand their collective understanding of how validity figures in nearly every teacherly move, insofar as the move is intended to probe for evidence of understanding. This involves coming to terms with the ways in which teaching and assessment intersect in practice—sometimes beneficially, as in skillful formative assessment on the spot, and sometimes detrimentally, as in too much practice testing.

These knowledge distribution problems may seem formidable—though only, we think, from the perspective of how U.S. schools have traditionally been designed—namely as cellular institutions. In fact, these problems are all learning problems—ones that schools can organize themselves to address—for example, by means of teacher learning groups, better materials curating, and collegial coaching. We have more to say about these strategies in our New Directions.

Efficiency

As we use the term in the context of data use in teaching, efficiency has to do with suiting the data system to the circumstances of practice. If the teacher is a teacher of English language learners and wants to track students' growth in reading, then—as one ELL teacher we interviewed told us—she cannot depend exclusively on the students' annual ELA state testing data (NYSESLAT in New York State). She needs other data, too, that tracks development more finely and offers her and her students more timely signals of the students' growth. So, for example, this teacher maintains folders on all her students. They include running record data, evaluated writing assignments, evidence of growth in managing text complexity, and anecdotal memos that she writes following every individual session with a student. This teacher can produce and manage such a data set efficiently because she works with her students one-on-one and in small groups. However, the 7th-grade ELA

teacher whose class this ELL teacher "pushes into" (to support some number of her ELL students there) cannot do the same. She works with so many
more students, and more often in large groups rather than one-on-one. Yet
she can still make a point every week of tracking at least one literacy indicator for every ELL student in her room—via a Guided Reading session
report, an exit ticket, an observation over the student's shoulder, or a deliberately elicited oral comment—and she can record these data and share
them with the ELL teacher.

We found that most of the practitioners we studied, even if they lacked
precision in describing validity and efficiency, seemed aware of the need for
both in data use in teaching. For example, one principal told us that "the
state testing gives you something more standardized," by which we think
he meant *valid*, "but I think," he added quickly, that "what is necessary is
to look at the specific tools, and see how reliable and viable they are"—by
which we think he meant *efficient*.

GENUINELY BIG DATA

We described, above, the difference between big-test data and intimate data,
but we also acknowledged that genuinely big data may also come to play
an increasingly important role in schooling (National Academy of Education, 2017). In fact, it is already playing a circumspect role. Even though
big data transactions in any field are still technically challenging, there is a
lot of talent available for dealing with the challenges—and no longer just in
advertising, sports, manufacturing, and science.

   Education Week's Benjamin Herold reports, for example, on an ambitious start-up called AltSchool, funded by $133 million of venture capital—
mostly from Facebook founder Mark Zuckerberg. AltSchool employs data
scientists and engineers to develop tools and other potential products for
future schools based on data generated by students learning now at the company's network of lab schools in the San Francisco Bay Area and New York
City. The data is collected by multiple devices embedded in the schools'
environments. These measure students' engagement levels, keystrokes, vocabulary use, eye movements, skill development, knowledge acquisition,
and more (Herold, 2016a; Herold & Doran, 2016). In this case, big data
is harvested and aggregated intimate data, often exceeding intimate data,
typically captured in online learning environments, and typically focused on
learning processes.

   However, as Andrew Ho (2017) points out, big data can also take the
form of massive administrative data (for example, data related to eligibility
for free or reduced-price lunch, gender, race, disability status, ELL status,
attendance, and, of course, personal identifiers like names and addresses).

And he notes that variables in one kind of big data can be linked to variables in another by means of unique identifiers. This is, of course, one basis of the promise that researchers and policymakers (and—yes—marketers too) see in big data. And, as Ho points out, it is also the basis of concern about big data as a potential violator of family and student privacy.

Indeed, it may be that innovations like AltSchool will at some point encounter political opposition based on privacy concerns. This is what happened to the educational big-data management company InBloom. That effort was also well-funded—with $100 million from the Bill and Melinda Gates Foundation and the Carnegie Corporation of New York. Its aspiration was to serve as a central data repository and analyst of student performance and other student data collected not only by districts and states but by vendors the districts and states work with. It aimed to encourage open-source tool development, to facilitate communication between vendors and districts, and to relieve districts and states of the enormous costs of managing and securing their own student data (Herold, 2014). However, within just over a year of its launch, InBloom disappeared under a storm of privacy concerns (Ho, 2017; National Academy of Education, 2017).

Meanwhile, it is important to note that privacy concerns are not the only threat to (and from) big-data projects, in education as elsewhere. The projects can also fail on efficiency grounds. Despite the validity they amass through sheer scale, big-data projects may nonetheless fail an efficiency test in dealing with what Atul Gawande (2009) calls the extreme complexity of practice at the ground level. He refers to medical practice, but we believe—and explain in the next chapter—that a similar level of complexity attends teaching practice too.

Science journalist Amy Standen (2014) tells the story of a big-data strategy involving the assemblage of a massive "electronic cohort" of pediatric lupus patients. Although the effort likely saved the life of a young lupus patient at Stanford's Lucille Packard Children's Hospital, as reported in the *New England Journal of Medicine* (Frankovich, Longhurst, & Sutherland, 2011), it is *not* routinely used today even at Stanford. Today, Standen reports, the hospital trusts in what it regards as the more efficient method of a small team of doctors conferring on the basis of their own relevant cases, their familiarity with ordinary experimental medical research, and their collaborative examination of the patient. There will likely come a day when they deal also with predictions and probabilities drawn from big data, though they will likely still include the other kinds of data in their deliberations—even perhaps giving precedence to them. In the end, efficiency depends on circumstances—what the situation demands at this moment, and what time and constraints on attention permit.

So it goes in educational contexts too, as educational researcher James Paul Gee argues in an interview with journalist Benjamin Herold. It is foolish, Gee says, to think that keystroke and chat window dialogue data captured in online courses, or biometric data on posture or skin temperature captured in gaming environments, are inherently more valid in describing or boosting learning than is the ordinary data that comes from simply observing and interacting with students as they learn (Herold, 2016b). Essentially, he asks, who would give precedence to the former over the latter? We would say that much depends on the *use* of the data. Do you want to predict massive patterns of behavior? If so, consult genuinely big data. But if you are a teacher, you are more likely interested in knowing how to help Jorge learn how to read. And intimate data is what you need for that. Indeed, as Ho (2017) suggests, genuinely big data may put you in exactly the wrong mindset—for example, a tacit presumption that Jorge is demographically a long-shot in terms of learning to read well.

SUMMING UP

More than 15 years ago, when Milbrey McLaughlin and Joan Talbert were conducting the voluminous research that informs their groundbreaking book, *Building School-Based Teacher Learning Communities* (2006), one teacher asked them, what *is* data? A teacher would not likely ask this question now. That's not just because the word *data* is ubiquitous generally now (for example, in the teacher's monthly personal media bills), but also because it has become ubiquitous in teaching. On the other hand, this chapter was designed with the idea in mind that the question is still very useful, and a reluctance to ask it is dangerous. Teachers cannot engage in thoughtful data use in teaching without knowing some of the distinctions that this chapter makes—as related, for example, to big-test data, intimate data, and genuinely big data; or to validity and efficiency in data use. The chapter also deals with the important question of what teachers talk about when they talk about data, and implicitly about what they *might* talk about. What follows is the first of the book's New Directions, which portrays a context for such talk.

Building a *Data-Wise* Culture in Every School

It is not enough to harbor knowledge of assessment at the district level, the consultant level, or even the school administration level. This knowledge and facility in using it has to be spread throughout a school in order to benefit students. Otherwise, as we saw in our research, big-test data can be misconstrued, and kids can be taken to be equivalent to their test performance bands ("my 1s and my 2s," as we heard a number of teachers say). And teaching itself, as well as crucial intimate assessments, can be displaced by big-testing look-alikes—for example, test prep worksheets or test prep online programs. But how do you spread solid knowledge of assessment and facility in using it throughout a school? Certainly, there is little evidence that recent state and district emphasis on using big-test data in evaluating schools and teachers—as consequential as this has been—has made teachers more knowledgeable about how to use it appropriately. So, if the state and the district can't make schools "data wise," then, who can? We argue here that only the school can. One reason is that only the school knows the people the data points to—namely, actual students who live in actual families that the school can get to know.

Data Wise is the title of a major resource we recommend to support this work at the school level. It is the 2013 book edited by Kathryn Boudett, Elizabeth City, and Richard Murnane. Its subtitle is *A Step-by-Step Guide to Using Assessment Results to Improve Teaching and Learning*. The book recommends that every school's instructional leadership team (with staff added as needed) be a data team too. Then, it says, this data team should:

1. Manage an inventory of the multiple sources of data available to the school
2. Solve technology challenges related to data use as these arise
3. Work to display data in practical and understandable ways
4. Help colleagues collect, organize, display, curate, and use more intimate data

This may sound like a lot of responsibility, but all four tasks listed above are essential. To get genuine and beneficial data use in teaching, someone has to take on these responsibilities, and in nearly all our schools, some*one* did. But the *Data Wise* authors urge schools to entrust these responsibilities to a team instead of some*one*, and they add one additional responsibility: they call on the team to share its assessment expertise as it grows with other colleagues. Jennifer Price and Daniel Koretz, coauthors of one of the *Data Wise* chapters, suggest that all educators need to understand several key assessment concepts, including validity, reliability, sampling and measurement error, and score inflation. These concepts apply in some fashion to intimate assessment too, but they are crucial to big-test assessment (Price & Koretz, 2013).

A good way, we think, to help a whole school get wiser about big-test assessment in particular, but also assessment more generally, would be to organize a faculty-wide read of the Price and Koretz chapter in *Data Wise*, and also of the classic essay by James Popham (2003), entitled "The Seductive Allure of Data," in which the author (a major figure in the field of psychometrics) offers a succinct guide to what can make any assessment—whether big-test or intimate—instructionally useful. The reading could be enhanced by simultaneous discussions of these texts in facilitated seminars at a whole-faculty meeting. And the school might go even further and engage in a book-club chain reading of Koretz's (2008) very accessible book about standardized testing, called *Measuring Up: What Educational Testing Really Tells Us*. In a book-club chain, one group of volunteers reads the book first and discusses it, then passes along copies of the book plus notes and questions from its discussion to a second volunteer group, and so on, until volunteers run out. Then all the volunteers (or a subset) plan a workshop for other colleagues.

In New York City, the term *data team* has been shaped historically not only by readers of *Data Wise* (especially the first edition which called for a data team separate from the school's instructional leadership team), but also by an initiative codesigned and launched in 2005 by an inventive partnership involving a New York school reform network, New Visions for Public Schools, and the School of Public Affairs at Baruch College. At one point, then-Chancellor Joel Klein required that every school in the city appoint a data team modeled on this initiative—scaling up much too rapidly a very successful pilot innovation. The fact that we found few remnants of these teams in the nine schools we studied may be a consequence of this too-fast scale-up, though we know that teams do persist in a number of the other roughly 1,800 city schools. Happily, in any case, a key shaper of the innovation, Nell Scharff Panero, and a researcher who worked with her to study the innovation closely, Joan Talbert, wrote about the pilot teams and their methodology in a book called *Strategic Inquiry: Starting Small for Big Results* (2013), a book that is also a great resource for efforts to support data use in teaching. It is especially valuable in two respects. First is the attention it calls to "starting small"—that is, tracking student learning intimately with the focus on skills or subskills that are demonstrably related to larger learning goals, and that show up (or ought to show up) in everyday samples of student work. Second is the attention it calls to a discourse that is crucial for recording teaching and for talking about it—one that puts aside judgmental observations and commentary and makes room for undefensive conversation. Panero and Talbert call it low-inference discourse, or low-inference transcription. As we explain in the Appendix, this is the kind of discourse we used in working with our research participants. We are particularly fond of research methods that travel well across practitioner and academic worlds—ones that both insiders and outsiders can use to communicate and grow in their mutual understanding. This is because we think that improving teaching and schooling demands insider–outsider partnerships.

Finally, we recommend one more reading to support a school's efforts to develop collective assessment expertise: Brent Duckor's and Carrie Holmberg's *Mastering Formative Assessment Moves* (2017). Even though the term "formative assessment" is in its title, the book implicitly challenges the idea that this is something *apart* from teaching. Their seven moves of formative assessment are clearly teaching moves too, and the authors encourage this association. A sprawling text for an individual read-through, it is a brilliant text for school-wide knowledge building. We imagine, for example, different colleagues assigned different moves, reading closely the chapter associated with their assigned move, videotaping their own and their colleagues' illustrations of it and spreading the exploration of the seven moves across a year of collective collegial learning.

CHAPTER 2

What Is Teaching?

In focusing on *teaching* in this chapter, we do not mean the practice as routinely used in nonschool settings—for example, in referring to how we teach our own children, or share with a friend some way of gardening or cooking. We use the word *teaching* as school teachers experience it. The word signifies a practice that unfolds over months within rooms typically crowded with young people—who in some cases stay there nearly all the school day, and in other cases rotate in and out on a fixed schedule. It is a practice marked by certain discernible behaviors that ride on a bed of churning dynamics. In this chapter, we explore the behaviors, though we start with the dynamics. This is not just because the dynamics help drive the behaviors, but also because they are often overlooked. And when policymakers, district and school leaders, or even teachers themselves attend only to behaviors when thinking about teaching, they can trick themselves into thinking that teaching can be learned more easily than it actually can be, practiced more smoothly than is typically the case, evaluated simplistically as either good teaching or bad teaching, and changed more readily than is often possible—for example, in response to data that suggests the need for change.

DEEP DYNAMICS OF TEACHING

In his 2011 book about teaching, veteran policy researcher David K. Cohen directly addresses the question of how teaching works at a deep level. He means the challenges that make it up, the ones that teachers must wrestle with in order to teach at all, and certainly in order to teach well. In the process, he draws on a tradition in thinking about teaching with key contributions from John Dewey (1899/1990), Willard Waller (1932), Phillip Jackson (1968), and Dan Lortie (1975). The tradition also includes more contemporary scholarship often influenced by Cohen—for example, Joseph McDonald (1992), Magdalene Lampert and Deborah Ball (1998), Anna Richert (2012), and Sharon Feiman-Nemser (2012). Cohen calls teaching's deep dynamics *predicaments*. Lampert (1985, 2001) calls them *dilemmas*, as does Richert (2012). McDonald (1992) refers to the subterranean space where the dynamics operate as a "wild triangle" whose interior angles (as defined by teacher, learner, and subject) are continuously changing (p. 1). Here, we use the more generic term, *deep dynamics*, to signify the relational movement in each of them, and its impact on teaching's surface behaviors. But all the names for these challenges suggest that they are hard to manage. And the naming helps in the management in that it gives teachers and their colleagues and coaches something to look for, reflect on, and talk about.

In our examination of teaching's deep dynamics, we rely especially on Cohen's (2011) and Richert's (2012) parsing, but we add insight too from another important tradition in the study of teaching, one that blossomed in the 1990s with first editions of pathbreaking books by Gloria Ladson-Billings (2009), Lisa Delpit (2006), Geneva Gay (2010), Sonia Nieto (2010), and others. This work called attention to the crucial role in teaching of cultural empathy and relevance.

We identify three deep dynamics, or challenges, in teaching:

1. Figuring out what to teach, not only in terms of planning teaching but also in performing teaching on the spot.
2. Understanding students as people and building relationships with them that are mutually respectful and beneficial.
3. Discerning what these students may already know and what they learn from the teaching they experience.

Before explaining these dynamics below, we offer a roughly 20-minute slice of teaching to ground the explanation. Extracted from one of our low-inference observations of teaching—in this case, within the 7th-grade classroom of Anthony Tandoc (AT) and Jose Luiz (JL). (As throughout the book, these teachers, once introduced, are subsequently referred to by the initials of their pseudonyms.) We have added to the original transcript some commentary to provide contextual details, plus a few higher-level inferences drawn from follow-up interviews and other observations of the same teachers.

A Slice of Teaching

It is just after lunch, and AT begins his opening lesson of the afternoon with a burst of energy expressed in both his hand movements and his voice: "All right, please open your notebooks. This is your prompt." He points to it on an electronic whiteboard, then pauses and adds, "Give examples from your life!" The prompt is a writing prompt focused on a text the students have previously read. Essentially, it asks the students to name and reflect on any of the text's key ideas as they relate to their own experiences. It is very early in September, and AT and JL are using these opening weeks to discover new things about their new students as readers and writers—in this case, whether the students can toggle between close textual references and accounts of personal experience.

"Kevin," AT asks in a classroom-wide voice, "how might you start your response to the prompt without repeating the words of the prompt?" As the student answers, AT types the answer verbatim, and it projects onto the whiteboard. His co-teacher, JL, offers another possible first sentence for responding to the prompt, and AT records and projects this one too. JL is a special educator who has been assigned to this class because roughly 40% of the students it serves have special needs requiring close attention.

> *AT:* It is now 12:27, and by 12:41 I need your responses. I want you to be able to answer this prompt. Kevin gave you one way to start, and Mr. L gave you one. You can also come up with one of your own. And remember to give examples from your life!

As the students tackle the prompt, AT roams the room, pausing to observe the writing, occasionally speaking quietly to individual students. JL does the same. Bending down to read one student's sentence, AT tells her in a very soft voice: "We don't do that. You don't need the three dots." And the girl erases her ellipsis. Because it is the beginning of the school year, AT seizes every opportunity he can to emphasize what "we do here" and what "we don't do here," in matters that range from passing papers to using certain conventions in writing. Over the next 10 minutes, AT and JL cover the room, peering down at writing in progress, sometimes commenting, sometimes answering writers' questions. As AT tells us later, he is "learning his students as writers," just as they are "learning" him as teacher, and close observation is one of both parties' learning tools.

> *AT:* [adjusting the time] You have two more minutes, let's go. Once it hits that 12:43 [with the countdown visible on the whiteboard], we'll share.

AT walks to the front right table and leans over the shoulders of the students there. Then at 12:43, he stands up straight and speaks to the whole class.

"Sit up, you just ate lunch. Now get that oxygen to your brains." Then, as he returns to the front desk, he adds, "Some of you have great responses. Let's share."

Meanwhile, JL prepares to record responses, again projected on the whiteboard.

> *AT:* [responding to a hard-to-hear first offering] Gotta speak up, you're mumbling. But I like your use of the word *think* there. Mr. L, let's put that word in bold!

The Content Dynamic

Everywhere beneath the surface of this brief slice of teaching, the content dynamic is pervasive. It underlies AT's and JL's choice of a writing prompt, one that aims to illuminate a key writing skill. It underlies their decision to scaffold the students' response to the prompt with two sample sentence stems (one from JL—likely planned in advance—and also one from a cold-called student), but with an invitation to come up with their own stem if they choose. And it certainly figures in AT's on-the-spot decision to say that he likes the word *think* in the first shared response. Of course, he also uses this comment to soften his criticism of the student's mumbling, but the admiration is not faint praise. This is a teacher with deep knowledge of writing and language, as we know from spending nearly 3 years in his classroom. When he says softly at the start of sharing that "some of you have great responses," he means exactly what he says, and implicitly commits to helping them figure out for themselves what bits of writing are great and why, and what are not yet great and why. This is typical of several moves he makes during the slice that not only exhibit his content sense, but also alert the students to how he plans to manage the second dynamic: building a mutually respectful and beneficial commitment.

The question of what a teacher should teach may seem a given to most nonteachers. The state decides this, right? Or the district? Or the textbook? Indeed, some people—including policy leaders, reformers, and parents—may expend political energy on insisting that the state adopt one set of standards over another, or the state or district one textbook over another. Most states and districts do in fact constrain what should be taught when and to whom, and most schools refine this further at the school-wide or grade-wide level. And the many materials that districts and schools purchase (including classroom libraries, online learning programs, and whole systems of literacy instruction with consulting coaches) add further constraint and prescription. But it is important to note that there is often much misalignment among these various sources of direction, even when the suppliers claim perfect alignment. And even if the sources are well-*enough* aligned, teachers need their own consistent internal content monitoring in order to make adequate decisions about scheduling, pacing, and emphasis, or to make thoughtful content adaptations to accommodate particular contextual factors and individual students' needs.

To make such finely grained content decisions, teachers must have a good working knowledge of the key ideas, questions, and tools of the domains that figure in their work. For a middle-school English teacher like AT, these domains include language, reading, writing, literature, and young adult literature—and in the schools we studied, history too. For a 4th-grade teacher, they include the younger varieties of all these things, plus math, science, health, and art. Teachers at both levels also need what Lee Shulman

(1987) famously called *pedagogical* content knowledge—that is, knowledge of how students typically learn content at a particular level, and knowledge of the misconceptions the students typically need to *unlearn*.

Ultimately, teachers are the main curators of the content they teach in most settings—even at schools that have strong teacher learning communities. Curating in teaching involves browsing for the best stuff one can find online and from other available resources, honing it in use, and storing it carefully for future use. Observing AT, one can spot considerable curatorial skills in action—for example, his deep familiarity with an extensive classroom library. Observing poor curators, by contrast, one can often spot ragged shards of content flying about the room.

The Mutual Respect and Commitment Dynamic

We know from an interview with AT that the lesson from which we excerpted the slice portrayed above was more than an exercise in writing from experience. He regarded it also as a data source to inform his emerging relationship with students who on this September afternoon were new to him. And he regarded it as self-affirmation for them as readers, writers, and learners. All these objectives were on his mind as he planned the class with his co-teacher, and as he circulated through the classroom to have brief private visits with many students. It animated his hearty lines to them, "This is *your* prompt!" and "Give examples from your life!"

Moreover, we learned as we continued to observe AT's practice that he continues throughout the year to learn his students, and not just as writers and readers, but as people with families, cultures, personal histories, interests, hopes, disappointments, mindsets, and sometimes traumas. A generation of deep thinkers about teaching—for example, Bill Ayers (2010), Lisa Delpit (2006), Geneva Gay (2010), Gloria Ladson-Billings (2009), Carol Lee (2007), Sonia Nieto (2010), and Pedro Noguera (2003)—have persuasively argued that teachers' deep attention to who their students are as people is their students' right. In making this case, they are especially alert to the ways that racial, cultural, and linguistic mismatch between teachers and students can undermine students' learning, and to how deliberate efforts by teachers to engage and connect with their students and the students' families and communities can head this off. Indeed, longitudinal research in highly poverty-impacted Chicago schools has shown, for example, that high measures of trust by families in their children's teachers is a key predictor of a school's opportunity to beat the odds that deep poverty lays on student achievement (Bryk, Sebring, Allensworth, Lupescu, & Easton, 2010). Building this trust depends especially on teachers' capacity to demonstrate *respect* in the way that Sara Lawrence-Lightfoot (2000) defines it—namely, as a force that "creates symmetry, empathy, and connection in all kinds of relationships, even those, such as teacher and student, doctor and patient, commonly seen as unequal" (pp. 9–10). It also depends on the teacher's implicit and explicit commitment to act in their students' best interests, and to follow through in discernible ways on this commitment.

AT offers several signs of respect during the teaching slice—ones that his students can easily spot. At roughly 12 years old, they are already knowledgeable readers of teachers. He offers them a choice of phrases to start off their writing, including one contributed by a classmate, and one the students may create for themselves. He times their work (a sign of his determination to make the most of their time), though he also adds a little slack to the timing so as not to rush them. And he conferences with them individually, briefly and quietly. He protects them all from mumbling, but simultaneously protects the mumbler from a loss of face—not only by noting a detail he admires in the student's writing, but by asking his co-teacher to type and project it in bold font. Perhaps most conspicuously, he and his co-teacher honor all their students' thoughts and words by projecting them for all to see. In their 2017 book about formative assessment moves, Brent Duckor and Carrie Holmberg call this "tagging," and attest to its power to boost learning.

Important as this is, note that the second dynamic is not just about building an environment of respect in the Ladson-Billings or Lawrence-Lightfoot sense. It is also about building an environment to support what Cohen (2011) calls mutual commitment. As carpenters do with wood and plumbers with pipes, Cohen writes that teachers work with students, though these "targets" of their work are quite unlike wood and pipes in their "cooperativeness." Yet every teacher's practice depends fundamentally for its success on students' inclination to cooperate in learning. It seems odd, given the portrayals in popular culture of children's and teenagers' recalcitrance toward adults, that this dynamic is not more widely understood. Indeed, even teachers themselves seem to think—quite apart from their students' degrees of buy-in—that they ought to be more successful than they are in affecting the students' learning. And policymakers are famously certain of it. And to cover up failure, teachers may refrain from pushing too hard. They may set their learning goals for students very low, or make implicit and sometimes explicit deals with the students: if you cooperate to a point, I'll agree to press you only so far (Powell, Farrar, & Cohen, 1985; Sedlak, Wheeler, Pullin & Cusick, 1986). AT is implicitly soliciting his students' agreement to a different kind of bargain, and it resonates in one of the first things he tells them: "It is now 12:27, and by 12:41 I need your response. I want you to be able to answer this prompt." There it is—as simple as possible. On the one hand, you must give me something. On the other hand, I am confident that in this giving, you will gain something.

At every moment, the teacher must choose how to interact with students across a broad spectrum—whether to speak, look, respond, invite, walk away, ignore, discourage, and so on—under the pressure that the students' willingness to cooperate is crucial to the teacher's success, *and also* on the understanding that the teacher's willingness to press is crucial to the students' success. As McDonald (1992) puts it, the teacher is continually inquiring, "What are they thinking and feeling—toward me, toward each other, toward the thing I am trying to teach? How near should I come? How far off should I stay? How much clutch, how much gas?" (p. 1).

But the teacher is not just inquiring. In all these moves, the teacher is also building an intimate environment that students may come to trust. This is how, as Theodore and Nancy Sizer (1999) assert, the adult keepers of school convince their students to accept the legitimacy of what may otherwise seem to them just another compulsory moral order in their lives.

The "Knowing What They Know" Dynamic

The third dynamic is, of course, the one that data use enthusiasts think of first, but some of them also think that most of the guidance in managing it comes from big-test data. For example, numerous school leaders interviewed in our study spoke as if they thought the biggest challenge in this area lies not so much in teachers gaining knowledge of their students' knowledge, but rather in higher-ups transporting this knowledge to teachers and persuading them to act on it. In most of our schools, both the pipeline and the persuasion was under the control of an assistant principal or other professional staff member called a data coach. In all cases, this was a person who had generally good big-test interpretation skills, and a knack for creating spreadsheets—particularly ones that record, student by student, test items that stumped them on the last standardized test. Sometimes these spreadsheets also included standardized intimate data too— for example, literacy scores on the Developmental Reading Assessment (DRA), a Pearson product that guides a teacher's one-on-one assessment of a child's reading level, accuracy, fluency, and comprehension.

Using the spreadsheets (either in grade-level teams or on their own), teachers were expected to match each identified deficit with a teaching intervention—for example, placement in a small reading group on a deficit-alike basis, or time allotted to an individualized online reading program. In Part II, Chapters 4–7, we present close-up images of this process. It is a very rational process, though it often misses the forest (actual reading and writing skills) for the trees (big-test items), and otherwise overdetermines what students know (or do not). And it overlooks what the teacher learns by working with the students on a daily basis. It misses the fact that this knowledge-in-action is at least as valuable and useful as big-test data and even intimate test data— even if the teacher does not record it.

During the teaching slice above, for example, AT moves from student to student across the entire room, and collects data in all corners, though he does not record it on the spot. In many instances, however, as we learned, he records it when he reflects at the end of the day. Meanwhile, of course, he and his teaching partner make a visible record, by means of their fast typing on a projected Google Doc, of what every student speaks aloud to the whole group. This is quite a contribution to what another teacher we interviewed described as the day-by-day "arc" of sense-making about students that every teacher builds, whether validly and sensitively or not. In fashioning this arc of sense-making, teachers puzzle over the signs of what their students know at this moment, as supplementary information to what a previous standardized test score or Tuesday's quiz may have told them, or to what a student's individualized educational plan (IEP), or a parent, or a push-in ELL teacher, or a colleague who also teaches the child may have told them. Ideally, the puzzlement ranges across such factors as the students' prior understanding and emerging understanding, and includes how they seem to think about what they know, and whether this thinking easily lends itself or not to gaining deep understanding.

Ultimately, of course, it is never enough for teachers to figure out for themselves what their students know. They must also share what they learn with the students. In the AT and JL classroom, students are asked to speak (not mumble) what they know for their *own* sake as well as the sake of others in the room. And what they know is often—as in the slice—immediately published on the whiteboard—which, by the way, absent students and even parents can access from home. Both teaching tactics are examples of what some scholars and practitioners call making thinking visible (Edwards, Gandini, & Forman, 2012; Krechevsky, Mardell, Rivard, & Wilson, 2013; Ritchart, Church, & Morrison, 2011). As it turns out, these tactics have as much to do with managing dynamic two as they do dynamic three. They confirm for students that their willingness to make an effort in proportion to their teachers' press increases their understanding bit by bit. In other words, the deal they've been willing to make with their teachers for mutual commitment pays off.

SURFACE BEHAVIORS OF TEACHING

Teachers dance on the shifting dynamics we portrayed above. Sometimes they dance with great dexterity and grace, and sometimes not. Most teachers have numerous routines in their repertoire. Within the content area we explore in this book, for example, these include group discussion of texts read in common; independent reading with conferencing; working in small groups or dyads on text interpretation or language problems; writing in response to prompts; and so on. But such routines are made up of simpler steps, and these steps are what we call teaching behaviors. In what follows, we explore four of them, illustrating these with brief images drawn from our research. We call the behaviors *pressing, pulling, asking,* and *walking away.* We treat them as discrete behaviors here for the purpose of exploring them in depth, but they actually overlap in use. For example, *asking* can involve *pressing*—though, as we discovered in our research, it too often does not. And, of course, these are not the only behaviors teachers use. Consider, for example, the overused behavior, *telling*.

Pressing

A growing emphasis on pressing has some roots in policymaking. The federal No Child Left Behind (NCLB) legislation, passed in 2002, declared that all children, across all the subgroups historically regarded as at risk of school failure—can and must reach state-determined levels of satisfactory competence in math and literacy by the end of the 2013–2014 school year. Of course, this deadline passed without the order's fulfillment, though this was not for lack of trying. And even in the aftermath (and the discrediting) of NCLB, and a like-minded successor called Race to the Top (see more about both and the larger policy context for data use in teaching in Chapter 3), an idea persisted in the U.S. that the biggest obstacle to high levels of achievement by all students is a refusal by many teachers to press for it. This is a vastly simplistic analysis. We do believe, nonetheless, that what some scholars call *academic press* is very important to effective teaching (Bryk, Sebring, Allensworth, Lupescu & Easton, 2010; Newmann & Wehlage, 1995). It can signify to students a commitment by their teachers to the students' best interests, and in the process (as in the second dynamic we explored above) inspire commitment from the students to work hard. Yet academic press is poorly distributed in U.S. schooling, and particularly scarce in schools serving poverty-impacted communities (Duncan & Murnane, 2011, 2014; Noguera, 2003; Oakes & Lipton, 2002).

We use the word *press* in contrast to what it may supplant—namely a spurious kindness or a genuine prejudice that expects too little of some students, and delivers too little to justify their literal confinement. And we use it to take note of some pedagogical techniques that have recently emerged—most of them originating in charter school networks that serve poverty-impacted students. Some of these networks have developed reputations for using press pedagogy to good effect. Doug Lemov (2015), managing director of one network, Uncommon Schools, has curated many of the press techniques developed in that network. Some of these have evocative names, like *cold call, no opt-out, stretch it,* and *100 percent.* Both his 2015 collection of these, and his 2016 book on literacy with Colleen Driggs and Erica Woolway, have proven useful and influential well beyond the charter sector, including in schools we studied. But press pedagogy—at least as we advocate it—is as much about attitude as technique. Indeed, when technique dominates, the pedagogy can lose its heart, and even turn Dickensian, more *shove* than press (Fisher, 2016; Taylor, 2016). From our perspective, press works well only if it maintains its balance on the dynamic of mutual respect and commitment where it is especially needed.

Here is how one of the teachers we studied pressed one day in introducing a writing prompt to her students. Notice the attitude here, the implicit confidence in her instructions and in her students. And though she uses the word *push*, she means what we call *press*, and she calls on the students themselves to make the move:

> Okay, you read, you heard, you talked [*steps in the lead-up to this assignment*]. Now we're going to take it to paper. And you're going to show my other class of 7th-graders, who will be assigned to read and comment on your papers, what you can do. Everybody, push yourself!

Other teachers among the ones we studied were less comfortable with pressing, and indeed, associated it with the more pejorative *pushing*. Here is how one teacher, Joanne Donilon (JD), who teaches English language learners put it in an interview with Joseph McDonald (JM):

> *JD:* I'm really pushing hard in ways that I never used to, and that feels uncomfortable.
> *JM:* Uncomfortable because you think it's unproductive?
> *JD:* I mean the jury's out, because I've only been doing this for a year and a half—pushing this hard. But it does feel that I'm pushing students to read and write at levels that are way beyond their reach. I used to spend a lot of time finding texts that were at the right level, that were engaging. Now it's more about pushing them to read texts that are in no way at a comfortable level for them. So, there's a lot of scaffolding and graphic organizers, and read and turn-and-talk discussion, and let's-jot-down-some-notes. But they're missing a lot. My instincts tell me that that is not really the right strategy, that the students are not identifying with this text, and that they're just muddling along and not getting much out of it.

JD's instincts may have been right, though we think in this instance—in the context of her school at this moment in time—that she was right to take the risk, namely, that she might press too hard. The school had lots of kindness but too little press. On the other hand, we did see some teaching across our study sites that clearly pressed too hard, although it was typically because the pressing was harsh in its tone, and the call for a partner in commitment too understated. Here's an example:

> The teacher has given his students a writing prompt with a footnote, and he calls attention to the footnote, "Now, why do I have 'text-based evidence' here? What's my purpose in pointing this out to you?"
> He cold calls a student named Martin who looks down and doesn't answer.

Then the teacher, turning from Martin and speaking to the whole class, erupts: "You guys have to retain. Go back to the rubric if you need help. You know the problem. I keep telling you guys this. You only have bits and pieces. When you can speak, you can write." Martin, hand on his chin, looks up but does not speak.

The teachers who are eager to press and the ones who are wary of it usefully define a continuum of variation that all teachers are wise to negotiate rather than resolve in any fixed way. The other behaviors we describe here can similarly be imagined along such continua. And in experimenting with all of them, it helps teachers to know that they are parties to a negotiation, and that there's no one good way to use a teaching behavior. So much depends on context. The good news, however, is that each use of a press gathers data—namely from the students themselves. What happens if I only press this far? What if I pressed really hard? What does it mean that Martin has looked up, but still not spoken? It also helps for teachers to have settings in which they can rehearse the continua among other teachers, and try out *this* much press versus *that* much. We did, after all, introduce this part of the chapter by comparing teachers to dancers who dance atop a set of whirling dynamics. And just as dancers need to rehearse with other dancers, and actors with other actors, experimenting with and then discussing some range of possible moves and emotions in a choreography or a script— teachers need to rehearse too. The teacher who cold called Martin needs a colleague to advise him that when you cold call someone, stick with him, help persuade him to commit to the work, don't turn him into an example for "you guys."

Pulling

Sometimes called conferencing, the pulling behavior seems to turn a crowded room into an intimate one-on-one encounter of teacher and student. Or at least it does if the teacher is practiced at creating the illusion. Here is how one of the teachers we studied described *pulling*:

> I pulled one of my kids today [in independent reading] who I noticed was reading something that looked to be a little above his reading level. At first, he told me that the book was super easy, but I asked him to talk privately with me about it, and he acknowledged that some of the words are hard. So, I'm like, "Well, let's go talk about it," and we sat down [in an improvised privacy], and I listened to him read and retell parts he understood, then asked him some comprehension questions. No clue. So that tells me this is a kid who outwardly wants to read and wants to do well, but doesn't have the stamina for it, and is making poor choices. He wants other kids to think that he is reading better than he actually is.

In this instance of pulling, a teacher inquires into what a single student can do on his own, and what he cannot do, and using the data she retrieves from the move, the teacher can plan a broader intervention. Pulling is often used also to investigate patterns of learning among multiple students. For example, one teacher told us that her students were doing relatively well on big-test assessments and also on so-called interim assessments designed to predict big-test assessment results. However, they were not progressing on their DRA assessments of independent reading. "I see how hard they work on their reading," the teacher told us, "so they *should* be showing more growth. That's something I want to go more into, and do a little conferencing about." The result of this kind of pulling may be a shift in broad teaching and assessment emphases—in this case, perhaps less focus on standardized testing (which has yielded inconclusive findings), and more focus on intimate assessments that may zero in on the suspected problem.

Pulling can be an intense experience, and a teaching move more powerful than a teacher may anticipate. One teacher we studied, Li Kai (LK), told Dana Karin (DK) about pulling a student to talk with her about a book the student had just finished reading independently. This is a routine in her teaching.

> *LK:* The book was *Freak the Mighty*, by Rodman Philbrick (1993), which resonates with so many kids—with its deeply rooted feeling of "I'm a freak, I'm insecure, there are all these things going on in my life that other people don't know about me." And it talks about how important friendship is, and it also lets kids empathize—I think in a way that a lot of them haven't tried before. I believe children can be very empathetic, but you have to teach them that it's OK, and here's *how* to talk about things empathetically. You can be empathetic and people aren't going to call you a weenie. You know? [Pause] So, anyway, at the end of this book last year, I had this kid crying [in a conference].
>
> *DK:* And what was that like for you?
>
> *LK:* I feel like *rewarding* is too basic a word. It was career-affirming. If I can do something to get kids to really feel deeply about a piece of literature and have that deep a reaction to it, and really want to talk about it, then I feel like I've done a good deed.

On the other hand, pulling—badly enacted—can be stigmatizing for students. In one classroom that we studied, the pulling seemed like a broadcast signal to all present indicating which students were "1s, 2s, or 3s" on the latest big-test prep results. Such a signal can cause a learning shutdown.

Asking

As we suggested above, asking is in many instances a form of pressing. Like other forms of pressing, it can be perceived by students or teachers as dangerous. David Kobrin (1992) begins Chapter 6 of his book about teaching with the following sentences: "The only crime that Socrates (ca. 470–399 BC) committed was asking questions of a lot of people—especially young people. For that, he was put to death" (p. 111). The questions that Socrates asked were perceived to probe too much, to push too hard, and to confuse or even embarrass the people to whom they were addressed. Today, teachers still encounter student resistance when they ask questions that press, probe, or confuse. This student resistance, combined at times with a teacher's fear of being drawn into unfamiliar terrains of content, can cause teachers to avoid asking what may seem to observers crucial follow-up questions, or cause them to ask mostly questions they have previously "taught" the answers to. Here is an observation transcript that includes both of these faults:

> *T:* What are "natural resources" [a reference to the text the students have read]?
> *S1:* Water.
> *T:* Do we get it in the store?
> *S2:* No, in rivers and lakes.
> *T:* Yes, natural resources come from nature. How did Native Americans get natural resources? Remember, they didn't have stores. So where did they get the natural resources?
> *S3:* Rocks.
> *S4:* Wood.
> *T:* One at a time. What about animals?

Both the student who answers "rocks" and the one who answers "wood" have uttered what the teacher determines (for some reason that seems to have more to do with her lesson plan than with the content involved) to be a wrong answer. The teacher seems in a hurry to establish a right answer, so she simply dispenses with wrong ones, and hints about the right one. In the process, of course, she discards an opportunity to learn about her students' thinking.

> *S5:* They looked at bulls.
> *T:* I want to share with you about this book. Drop your pencils. I need your undivided attention. Everyone sit up straight. Look up! [She begins reading from the text.]

Here, the teacher completely ignores what seems to her too odd an answer. She feels she cannot stop to ask, "Jason, what do you mean, 'They looked at bulls'?"

> *T:* [reading] "The tribes were thriving." What does *thriving* mean?

S2: They were angry?

T: You're on the right track. You're using your context clues. You're working hard. But if you're *thriving*, that means you're doing well. Now, put your pencil in your hand. While I'm reading, I want you to write down any examples of how the Native Americans were *thriving*.

S5: Actually, it was buffalos. [This comes from Jason who previously talked about bulls].

T: Okay, so whenever you hear about *thriving*, I want you to write it down.

The teacher ignores Jason again. There may be a good reason why—for example, because she may be trying to discourage a habit he has of making inappropriate remarks. But is this an inappropriate remark—even if ill-timed? Couldn't she have in this instance thanked Jason for correcting a previous utterance?

In our study, some of the best asking we observed happened within the context of pulling. The intimacy of pulling—well carried off—seems to make a difference in terms of teachers' courage to probe, as does the pursuit of specific data relative to a particular student's comprehension, interest, problem, and so on. One teacher told us simply, "As a teacher, I'm constantly asking students why they're doing what they're doing. I'm asking them to give me rationales to justify the decisions they make while they're reading or writing." In short, he is asking them to engage in metacognition, a very useful thing to do while learning. As we eavesdropped on such asking, we heard questions like "What are you reading? Why did you choose that reading? Why did you start with this detail? Where are you going next in this project? Why do you think that [such and such a character] said [what the student just read aloud]? What are you working on here?" Such questions are open to multiple responses, and well-anchored in some task at hand. They can provoke new thinking, raise other questions, or start a rich conversation. We also saw some good asking in the writing prompts we heard or read, and in a teaching activity whose frequency in the schools we studied surprised us: prompts for students to self-assess or peer-assess a piece of writing, or plans for writing.

By contrast, some of the worst asking we observed happened in what teachers typically call whole-class discussions—where asking is the central pedagogical tack, and is often preplanned, but where it typically occurs after engagement with a text. Here the asking was often *too* preplanned, rigid, and delivered in the ubiquitous IRE pattern (teacher *Inquires*, student *Responds*, teacher *Evaluates* the response), which, as John Goodlad (1984) pointed out in *A Place Called School*, results in a teacher out-talking a whole class of students by at least a ratio of 2 to 1. It was in whole-class discussions where (as in the example above) we observed teachers:

- Failing to ask follow-up questions (for example, about bulls and buffalos) that seem to scream for follow-up

- Fishing for specific answers they had planted (for example, "Natural resources come from nature")
- Bizarrely misleading students in the on-the-spot feedback they provided (for example, "You're on the right track" when the student thinks *thriving* means being angry)

Finally, whole-class discussions are where the teacher and students sometimes seemed to be operating in different zones of discourse, as in the following example:

T: [In reference to the title of a text they are discussing] Okay, why do they call them the "Northeast Indians"?
S: They lived in the Northeast.
T: Beautiful! Do *we* live in the Northeast?
S: No!
T: Yes, we do. Remember, we talked about the cardinal and intermediary directions?

None of these New York 4th-graders thought of themselves as living in the Northeast, though, of course, they might have meant that they do not live in the 16th-century Northeast or some other misconstrued place. A quick ask could have clarified this—for example, "Can anyone tell me where you think we *do* live, using directional words like *Northeast*?" However, the teacher doesn't ask this. She thinks that their confusion merits a simple reminder about something she has taught them before, something she believes can help them discover on their own the wrongness of their answers. She leaves the task of figuring out "northeast-ness" to the children themselves and whatever recollection they may have of her lesson on the "cardinal and intermediary directions," and she walks away.

Walking Away

Obviously, as in the example above, walking away can signify abandonment. However, it can also be an effective strategy under the right circumstances. In other words, this behavior can be expressed and experienced along a continuum—one that teachers can rehearse. Indeed, one of the middle-school teachers we studied told us that his faculty had determined that walking away is a crucial teaching behavior, and that they now work hard at cultivating its proper use:

A lot of us, including me, what we noticed when we visited each other's classrooms was just teacher talk. We weren't creating an environment where students were able to validate their own experiences [in talking with each other]. The teacher became the focal point of all knowledge—which we know is not true. This happens in high school, it happens in college. But we wanted to make sure that our kids were able to talk things through.

So the faculty agreed to rehearse a kind of pedagogy that starts off assertive—for example, a project prompt, followed by a demonstration—then withdraws deliberately to a monitoring stance.

> It's funny, because now my kids are like, "You don't teach us anything." I mean it's just a joke that we have going on, but I'm pretty proud of just being able [at times] to be the facilitator.

All four of the teaching behaviors we explore in this chapter require skill and discipline, but perhaps walking away requires the most. It is based on the idea that sometimes teachers teach best in the moment when they smartly disengage—for example, when they set an engaging problem, then leave small groups of students to solve it without their teacher's continual intervention; or when they allow students to engage in their own interpretations of a reading *before* they direct any "discussion questions" toward them.

At one point in our study, another teacher we studied thanked us for illuminating in our low-inference transcripts some teaching moments when he *ought* to have walked away, but didn't. Another teacher explained that her walking away was a method of pushing responsibility for good work down to students themselves—and, indeed, this is how we now define this key behavior, though it took us time to understand this. We saw the teacher assiduously train her students to work effectively with each other as reviewers of work in progress. This seems to us one of the environmental conditions that can make walking away effective. It can also encourage a heterogeneous group of learners to help each other. At one point, this teacher explained to us the impact on one child:

> Lawrence is a very special case. He has substantial disabilities, and can barely write or read. But the culture of the classroom is that his tablemates will take notes for him. Then I'll come by and check in. I'll do work for him as well. He does the mental processing while I do the writing because he can't do both at the same time.

Walking away requires preparation. One teacher told us that he uses rubrics to guide his students' learning and peer coaching. He asks students to translate the rubrics into their own language, and once they "own" this language, he uses it in lieu of the original language. Then he trusts the students to use the rubrics to monitor each other's projects as they develop.

Midway through this process, he supplies his own ratings as a corrective, and discusses with the class the trends he perceives in the development of their projects. This feedback cycle goes on for several weeks on the assumption that it is teaching and learning in progress, not just assessment. Then, in the end, the teacher engages in individual conferencing (that is, pulling) with each student, and enters a summative grade in his gradebook.

As with pressing, pulling, and asking, walking away can be dangerous. What if the groups do not understand the task? What if they think the teacher cannot be called back? What if, *in fact*, the teacher cannot be called back, and that for him or her, the walking away is deliberately or inadvertently dismissive instead of expectant. And what if the students regard the walking away as an abdication of teacher commitment—not in the joking way as one teacher quoted above put it, but in a serious way? On the other hand, a reluctance to ever walk away is dangerous too, and we found this reluctance in some of the teachers we studied. They seemed to feel that they always needed to *be there*, to hover over learning—which usually meant interrupting students' engagement with incessant commentary.

SUMMING UP

We think that all four of the teaching behaviors we explored above are essential components of teaching, though they are not the only behaviors worth using. Moreover, they require discretion in their use, and thoughtfulness in their combining.

- ***Pressing*** demonstrates a teacher's competence and determination to use the competence to benefit students—though a wrong tone can turn press to shove.
- ***Pulling*** demonstrates the teacher's caring about learners' individuality, though it can stigmatize students if done poorly.
- ***Asking*** demonstrates the teacher's willingness to travel into students' own worlds of thinking and knowing, but it requires a lot of background knowledge on the teacher's part to make the travel useful.
- ***Walking away*** demonstrates teachers' confidence in their own work and in their students' capacity for achievement, though it can also signal a lack of interest in both.

To use these behaviors successfully—that is, with optimal benefit to students' learning—teachers need to be mindful of the dynamics that underlie them. These involve swirling content, shifting signals of respect and commitment, and struggles to understand what students understand. In other words, as we put it metaphorically, teachers need to dance well on a moving floor. This is why we advocate that they rehearse their teaching regularly. There is more about rehearsing teaching in the New Direction that follows.

Learning to Rehearse Teaching

Versatility in teaching requires what some scholars have begun to call a rehearsal culture for teachers. Picture small groups of colleagues trying out particular teaching moves—coordinated conceptual, emotional, vocal, and physical moves—then discussing the results with each other. This implies the presence of a teacher learning community, one outfitted with norms that make it safe to rehearse—the equivalent for schooling of a company in theater or dance. Rehearsing teaching, like rehearsing a play or a dance performance, encourages the generation of multiple representations, and multiple possibilities uncovered in follow-up conversations. A school worried about unproductive whole-group discussion, for example, might decide to introduce and rehearse other kinds of whole-group pedagogy—for example, total-participation techniques (Himmele & Himmele, 2011), or other discussion formats like student-led ones (Novak, 2014). Or it might decide to rehearse and discuss open-ended discussion questions, cold-call questions, and follow-up questions.

As a rehearsal culture develops in a school, according to our Spencer colleague Ilana Horn (2010), it can cultivate the power to discern and tolerate complexity, build a readiness to reach beyond what one knows for sure, and create capacity for "data-oriented reasoning" (p. 255). In David Allen's book, *Powerful Teacher Learning: What the Theatre Arts Teach about Collaboration* (2013), he also emphasizes the *data* in rehearsing. He suggests that rehearsals engage in both "fast creation" and "slow creation." He associates the first with what theater directors Anne Bogart and Tina Landau (2005) call the "exquisite pressure" of an on-the-spot improvisational skit. For example, the director asks Jose and Lisa to confer for only a minute, then use only a chair and silence to fast-create an image of waiting. And Allen associates *slow creation* with the emergence over numerous conversations, improvisations, and experimental readings of, say, a new production of *Waiting for Godot.*

Thus, teachers who rehearse teaching—for example, as part of a schoolwide inquiry into the use of questioning—might fast-create a short video of lessons with questions drawn from a small sample of classrooms—not unlike some of the transcript excerpts we included in Chapter 2 as examples of "asking." Then the group can follow up with a discussion about what they see and hear in the video. This discussion—plus later videotaping, reading, observing, and transcribing in low-inference ways—might then slow-create guidelines for schoolwide practices in questioning.

CHAPTER 3

What Is Data Use in Teaching?

Following the basic questions explored in Chapters 1 and 2 (What is data? and What is teaching?), this chapter adds a final basic question in preparation for some deep dives into particular schools: What is data use in teaching? Our answer, simply put, is that it is an innovation which for the last half-century has been working its way through a complex educational system. It was inspired by broadly held if vaguely articulated beliefs about the role of equity in education, and the usefulness to education of efficiency strategies imported from other fields—in this case, an intensive focus on data. Typically, this innovation has been advanced as a means of improving educational outcomes for all students, including students impacted by poverty. And the forms it has taken have shifted in the course of its travels through the system. For example, as we explore below, it became a law spun out in policies and rules at federal, state, and school-district levels. In cities like New York, it became a strategy for devolving school reform powers to the school level. In the vast educational marketplace, it became "data-driven" products for sale: assessment systems, curricula, professional development regimens, and technologies. In schools, it became data coaches, data teams, spreadsheets, and value-added teacher evaluations. And in classrooms, it became rubrics, test prep, interim testing, online remedial programs, and more. In some classrooms, the innovation turned students into 1s, 2s, 3s, or 4s (named after their big-test performance bands), while in other classrooms, it granted students a greater sense of agency in their own growth.

James Spillane and his colleagues have identified this process of innovation sprawl as a form of tight coupling between classrooms and external sources of influence (Spillane, Parise, & Sherer, 2011). They take an idea of how schools have often resisted policy changes by means of *loose coupling*—that is, sealing off teaching practice in cellular classrooms (Weick, 1976); and they suggest that a recent generation of school reformers has learned how to reverse-engineer the process. Indeed, their claim seems undeniable. Few teachers today operate in the formerly widespread cellular way. They do not get to define independently what they teach. They do not get to operate alone behind closed doors. They are guided by state standards coupled with standardized tests, and with classroom observations and evaluations informed by testing results. And they are guided also by a vast marketplace of standards-oriented curriculum packages. The entire apparatus is designed to direct what teachers teach and to ensure that they follow the directions. Even a school's organizational routines—for example, the kinds of meetings it holds (say, to write curriculum together, or to evaluate student work samples together)—may serve as a coupling mechanism, tying the school's classroom instruction to government regulation (Spillane et al., 2011). From the perspective of our study, the effects of such coupling depend on whether it is expected to work magic. The schools we studied that tried *merely* to align themselves to the innovation as articulated in policy hand-downs, ended up being what we call weak implementers—that is, not effective data users. Meanwhile, the schools that expressly considered both policy demands *and* school needs, adjusting each by the light of the other, ended up strong implementers; that is, thoughtful data users.

THE INNOVATION'S THEORY OF ACTION

Implementing any innovation successfully—including data use in teaching—requires successive alteration of the innovation's implicit intentionality—that is, what it sets out to do and how. Of course, an innovation cannot actually *set out* to do anything. Intentionality can only be ascribed to people who promote the innovation, and who assist it along its journey. Policy analysts like Chris Argyris and Donald Schön (1996) call the successively constructed intentionality of an innovation its *theory of action*. The components of a theory of action include the following:

1. Clearly articulated but evolving goals
2. Specifications of planned steps
3. Elicitation of a stream of evidence regarding impact
4. Adjustments of the goals and steps based on analyses of this evidence

The problem with data use in education, as Andrew Ho (2017) points out, is that few of its champions bother to assemble this package. That is, they fail to articulate and manage the innovation's theory of action. This includes a number of the educators we portray in this book who turned out to be magical rather than adaptive users. One reason is that they themselves received the innovation from "higher-ups" in the system who instilled in them a great sense of urgency, but little sense of how the innovation was meant to work, and few models of its actual working. As Ho points out, "data in and of itself do not improve practice, unless they can answer relevant questions that participants in the process are asking, and with answers that inform subsequent actions" (p. 13). This cycle of question raising and answering at each level of use involves what Argyris and Schön (1996) (as well as other analysts of complex innovations) call *reframing* (Bolman & Deal, 1997; Coburn, 2006; Fischer, 2003; Goffman, 1974; McDonald, 2014; Schön and Rein, 1994; Snow & Benford, 1992). To reframe an innovation is to see it freshly as it enters a new context within some larger system. Innovators often think of this as a threat to the integrity of the innovation—and, indeed, it can sometimes be one. However, when an innovation like the one we explore in this book aims to operate across a massive system, the only way to ensure its integrity (in terms of purpose and impact, if not design) is through continual reframing. This can ensure that the innovation does not crack for want of adaptation to contextual circumstances, or dissolve into a mere slogan for want of any fidelity. The reframing helps the champions of such an innovation identify and preserve essential features, even as they investigate and determine how these should evolve across contexts and levels of use. So, for example, teachers who have received data reports that refer to the students they teach in terms of four big-test performance bands must reframe this information by juxtaposing it with intimate data about, for example, the students' language backgrounds, their self-assurance, the signs of their academic strengths and interests, and more. They must *not* treat the big-test information as the state or even the district must—namely, as a distant mirror of achievement gains (or drops) at the school overall. Otherwise the teachers risk working with their students as if the students were ciphers rather than the real people they see and work with. Similarly, data coaches or assistant principals who work at the border between district and school have to reframe the data they retrieve from an inbox or an intranet. They have to see it differently than the testing contractor who sent it to them did. They have to see it with a school's teachers, students, and families in mind. How can these stakeholders put it to good use, and how can school data leaders help them do this?

In the rest of this chapter, we trace the innovation we call data use in teaching from its putative beginning in a congressional hearing room, through layers of policymaking at federal and local levels, through a bustling marketplace of "data-driven" products for sale, and finally into practice. Here, we examine the practice of a middle-school team actively struggling with the poverty that menaces the school's children, and then the practice of an elementary classroom teacher struggling with the same menace among younger children. As it turns out, the team's work and the teacher's reflection on her work are expressions of the same hope. The hope is that the innovation we are exploring can somehow actually do what it was invented to do—namely, make a beneficial difference in the learning of poverty-impacted children.

ORIGINS OF U.S. DATA USE IN TEACHING

We trace the idea of data use in teaching to a set of hearings in the U.S. Senate Subcommittee on Education in 1965, focused on a bill that would become the first iteration of the Elementary and Secondary Education Act (ESEA). At issue in its passage was ESEA's Title I, which for the first time would provide federal funding to support the education of children from low-income families.

Elementary and Secondary Education Act

The mood on Capitol Hill then, as Milbrey McLaughlin (1974) tells the story, was self-congratulatory in expectation of ESEA passage. This would be a breakthrough, after nearly a hundred years of advocacy for and opposition to federal funding for schools (Beadie, 2016). The advocacy had been spurred by a belief, which spread widely in the post–World War II U.S., that education could redress inequality based on race and income, though only if the federal government took the lead. Meanwhile, the opposition was stoked by fear of the disruptive local impact if the federal government did indeed take the lead (Cohen & Moffitt, 2009).

The underlying tension between these perspectives first arose in the construction of the U.S. Constitution, and has figured in every major political event in U.S. history, from the creation (and later abandonment) of a national bank to the fate of the Affordable Care Act. By 1965, however, other federal legislation, notably the Civil Rights Act of 1964, had faced up to and beaten back (to some extent) even stiffer opposition on the same grounds.

At the time of these hearings, the bill had already passed the House, and Senate passage seemed assured. However, the very influential junior Senator from New York, Robert Kennedy, a presumed supporter, let it be known that he could not vote for the bill in what was then its current form. He was concerned that the billion dollars about to be given to districts would never reach the bill's intended beneficiaries—namely children impacted by poverty, particularly those attending segregated schools. At one Senate hearing on the bill, he said somewhat disingenuously, "I wonder if we couldn't have some kind of system of reporting. . . some testing system that would be established [through] which the people at the local community would know periodically as to what progress had been made under this program" (U.S. Congress, 1965, p. 514). In fact, behind the scenes, Kennedy's staff had already been assured by Johnson administration officials that the Senator would get what he wanted—though it would be years before a "testing system" was involved. As Samuel Halperin, then the Assistant U.S. Commissioner of Education for Legislation, told McLaughlin, what the Senator wanted was an evaluation with "numbers and figures" (McLaughlin, 1974, p. 3). What he actually got was the first evaluation requirement ever attached by Congress to a major piece of social legislation. In effect, Kennedy had turned an argument about federal aid to education as a spur to equality into an argument about data as a spur to equality.

Early Title I reports, however, as McLaughlin (1974) writes, "were little more than public relations documents," full of anecdotal knowledge useless to federal analysts, and presumably to parents too (p. vi). In her paper, she explores the reasons why: an infatuation then with novel kinds of evaluation; persistent resistance among educators to evaluation in general and standardized testing in particular; and continued opposition to federal involvement in education. Of course, the latter two aversions remain powerful factors still in U.S. educational policymaking. And so does Kennedy's evaluation requirement. Indeed, dissatisfied with the initial Title I evaluations, Congress mandated student performance reporting in 1974, and most states met the mandate by turning to commercially developed, norm-referenced, standardized tests. Daniel Koretz (2008) calls this a turning point in the history of standardized testing—or as we might put it in this book, in the rise of big-test data. Then in subsequent years, across multiple ESEA reauthorizations, the connection between standardized testing and ESEA grew stronger.

No Child Left Behind

In the late 1990s, a major political understanding was reached across parties and constituencies just in time for the reauthorization of ESEA, by a Democratic Congress in the first year of Republican President George W. Bush's administration. The understanding was that school reform could not only remedy poverty, but could also save the U.S. economy from the impact of globalization (Marshall & Tucker, 1992; McDonald, 2014; Resnick & Wirt, 1996). And big-test data could lead the way. No Child Left Behind (NCLB), the new version of ESEA, crystallized what had by then become widespread strategies of educational policymaking and reform—the use of standards, standardized testing, and sanctions for schools that fail to meet the standards.

What Senator Robert Kennedy thought of as auditable facts and figures to reassure community people had become in NCLB a sweeping dictate. All states would be required to test *all* students in grades 3 through 8 (and at least once in high school) in both literacy and math. They would report the test data to their states and then to Washington disaggregated by traditionally at-risk subgroups (Black, Hispanic, economically disadvantaged, students with disabilities, and students with limited English proficiency). The states would set explicit achievement targets for these subgroups, based on their own standards, and ratchet up the targets every year until *all* students in the state were proficient in literacy and math according to the states' own standards of proficiency. But *full*—one might say *perfect*—proficiency would be achieved no later than the 2013–2014 school year. Finally, the states would apply sanctions to schools that failed to meet yearly targets in *any* of the subgroups in any of the preceding 10 years. These sanctions (preset under the law) would range from warnings to declarations of school failure, school takeover, and school closure (Rhodes, 2012).

Today, the law's timeline seems absurd as does its insistence on perfection. Still, the NCLB coalition of expectation stayed intact for many years—indeed, years after this particular reauthorization of ESEA was due to expire, and after sanctions had escalated to a point where it looked like all schools in the United States might soon be declared failures. Meanwhile, many studies of NCLB found few real achievement gains under the law. Reading and math scores on the National Assessment of Educational Progress (NAEP) did rise slightly between 2003 and 2013, but they fell between 2013 and 2015. And though all the subgroups tracked under the law rose and fell with this pattern, the disparities among them remained or increased. For example, the achievement gap by poverty grew from 14.2 points in 2003 to 20.9 in 2015 (McDonald, Fraser, & Neuman, 2016; Sparks, 2016).

David Cohen and Susan Moffit (2009) make a strong case that NCLB—and indeed ESEA more generally, as well as other federal policymaking aimed at enhancing equality in schooling—have underestimated the complexity of schooling and teaching. We agree, and we think that these federal initiatives have also overplayed their hand politically. They have tended to press too hard from a distance, and to disregard too much the need for local discretion, local capacity building, and local reframing. We think that they also underestimated the impact of poverty.

Yet even as federal policymakers acknowledged what seems the folly of NCLB, and blamed political gridlock for the failure to dismantle it, few challenged its theory of action. Indeed, while offering states exemptions from the law's sanctions in its final years, President Barack Obama ratcheted up some elements of this theory of action:

- Not just high goals, but national ones
- Not just standardized testing, but a federally devised system of standardized testing
- Not just efforts to ensure high-quality teachers, but the use of bigtest student data in determining high quality

To achieve the exemption, states had to adopt college and career readiness standards—with the only available ones being the Common Core State Standards (CCSS), a national initiative thinly disguised as state-based (McDonald et al., 2016). States also had to adopt an assessment system capable of measuring attainment of the standards—with the only available ones being the two that the Obama administration had partly financed the development of. In addition, states also had to incorporate students' results from these assessments into teachers' and principals' evaluations.

The result of Obama's offer was temporary relief from NCLB in some states, and backlash against federal intrusion in many others. Eventually, even New York State, which had enthusiastically backed the CCSS and the new assessment system, backed away from both—following a major campaign by teachers and parents and a 20% boycott of standardized testing in 2015 and 2016 (albeit, interestingly, a boycott embraced mostly by middle-class parents).

In 2015, Congress finally passed a reauthorization of ESEA, 6 years overdue. Called the Every Student Succeeds Act (ESSA), the new law repealed much of NCLB, including the student achievement targets, the school sanctions, and federal involvement in teacher evaluation. And it added some opportunities for local experimentation that may prove beneficial—though it is still too early to know.

DATA USE IN TEACHING IN NEW YORK CITY

Constitutionally, of course, education is not principally a federal responsibility but a state one. Moreover, states typically devolve most authority for directing educational efforts to school districts—in the case of our study, the New York City school district. For many years, this district further devolved much of this authority to community school boards and superintendents. In 2002, however, a new system of control began to emerge under Mayor Michael Bloomberg and his long-serving Chancellor Joel Klein. It substituted a lean and data-focused New York City Department of Education, and a set of nongeographical support networks for schools, with a number of these operated by not-for-profit organizations rather than by the district itself. Principals got to choose their school's network. Even more importantly, they gained far more hiring control than before, and far more budget control and purchasing power than before (after a brief period of tighter city control over curriculum). This fundamental structural change was combined with a cultural one involving a heavier emphasis than before on student performance data collection and reporting at the school level, including the introduction of interim standardized testing to gauge readiness for high-stakes standardized testing, and serious accountability by the numbers that included principal terminations and school closures.

One element, introduced as the centerpiece of Mayor Bloomberg and Chancellor Klein's ambition for data use in New York City schooling, was a technology innovation called ARIS (acronym for the Achievement Reporting and Innovation System). ARIS cost $95 million, including cost overruns. For his part, the mayor wanted to provide the city's schools the equivalent of what he had provided the city's financial services industry as founder of the data and communications giant (and vendor) Bloomberg LP (McDonald, 2014; O'Day, Bitter, & Gomez, 2011). In a larger sense, ARIS symbolized New York City's reputation in the first decade of the

21st century as the leader in U.S. urban school reform, particularly with regard to knowledge management or the imported-from-business effort to use data to help people work smarter together (McDonald, 2014).

ARIS housed the latest state test results and previous years' achievement and attendance data for all students in the city, and results from a menu of customizable and no-stakes interim tests designed to mimic the state tests. It also housed a curated collection of teaching and learning materials, as well as links to other resources, and a set of powerful analytic and reporting functions, as well as blogging and wiki functions. Finally, it provided parents access to their children's school records in 10 different languages (Gold et al., 2012; Siman, Goldenberg, & Gold, 2014).

Originally built by IBM, then turned over to Wireless Generation (later known as Amplify), ARIS seemed very 21st century, circa 2006. Predictably, however—for the early 21st century—it seemed antiquated to some users not long after its launch in 2008, even after initial technical glitches were fixed. One reason, according to a study of ARIS usage in 2010–2011 by researchers from the Research Alliance for New York City, was that the database lacked real-time data, for example:

- Recent grades and attendance data
- Updates on student behavior
- Information from students' most recent Individualized Education Plans (for students with disabilities)
- What we call in this book intimate data, that is, data collected on a regular basis by classroom teachers—for example, with regard to reading skills (Gold et al., 2012)

In effect, the RANYCS survey and interview respondents complained that ARIS lacked reciprocity. Users could download data, but not upload it. One of the teachers we interviewed later referred to the absence in ARIS of "lively" data.

Some of the RANYCS respondents said they would also like to see family background data added to ARIS (Gold et al., 2012). Of course, obtaining family background data, let alone including it in ARIS, would likely have provoked challenges on privacy grounds, and lots of political backlash, especially in a city where there was, at the time, much tension between Mayor Bloomberg and neighborhoods where most of the city's poorest families lived and went to school. Still, the expressed need for such information among the surveyed ARIS users does reflect the original grounding of the innovation we're tracing as an instrument in a struggle against poverty.

Meanwhile, RANYCS researchers also found that the more sophisticated (beyond simple data retrieval) components of ARIS—the analytical and knowledge management functions (blogging and wiki)—were very much underutilized (Gold et al., 2012; Siman et al., 2014). This may be because, by 2010–2012, many users had other means of analyzing and communicating data, including ones less subject to district surveillance via click stream data counts. Certainly, by the time of our study, 2 years later, this was the case. Most of our schools were using Google Docs, G Suite, Excel spreadsheets, and a burgeoning generation of commercially developed school-based and cloud-based data management systems.

It was also true, by then, that the district had undergone yet another structural shift—a deliberate redisruption—back to community school districts. This was, again, the result of a mayoral transition, following the election of Mayor Bill de Blasio in 2013. This time, however, the shift proved less disruptive at first. That is, the genie of school independence—albeit monitored heavily by data—could not be quickly rebottled. For one thing, New York schools had grown used to deciding on their own what their curricula should be, with whom they should network for professional development purposes, with whom they should partner for social services and after-school programming, and what technologies and other materials they should purchase. And in the escalating emphasis on the CCSS and data use in teaching, they had also grown used to an expanding marketplace—one in which principals and school faculties were the chief shoppers. Indeed, as we studied data use in our nine schools from 2012 to 2015, we marveled at the scale of this "materials" marketplace, and grew very interested in its impact on the schools. We jokingly referred to it as the "material world," after a phrase in a Madonna song (Brown & Rans, 1984).

TEACHING IN A MATERIAL WORLD

Throughout our analysis of data, we coded for references in interviews to elements of "the material world," and we got lots of them—69 discrete referents in all, with some mentioned by multiple interviewees across multiple schools. It is important to add here that in our interview protocols, we did not call special attention to materials. The references were by-products of other questions we asked about data use, though we quickly noted material-world references as they occurred, and we sometimes followed up with additional questions.

In a second stage of analysis, we researched each of these 69 references. Most were to commercially available products (for example, *ReadyGen*, a literacy program from Pearson, or *Jumprope*, a data management tool), or to sources of multiple products (for example, *Teachers College Reading and Writing Project [TCRWP]*, or *Google*—both of these abundantly cited). However, some references were to generic tools available from multiple sources—for example, "running records" to diagnose individual students' reading skills and needs, or "protocols" to facilitate professional meetings to discuss data. We included such references in our material-world count only if they had a traceable commercial provenance. Then there was also an outlier group of references—where there was a clear commercial source, but where the person making the reference seemed to misunderstand the provenance. We took this as a sign that the material world is no more exclusively rational than any other dimension of data use in teaching that we write about. That is, references to elements of it can float across the environment like free radicals, and pop up in sometimes incongruous contexts.

We sorted the 69 material world referents into six groups:

1. Assessment materials and tools (14)
2. Culture tools—that is, ones relevant to installing a culture of data use in a school (7)
3. Curriculum materials (19)
4. Data management tools (5)
5. Professional development tools (21)
6. Technology tools that deal with teaching rather than with assessment or curriculum (3)

Finally, we distinguished between referents to relatively simple "tools" like a book about writing workshops or a handheld device for tracking student participation, to more complex ones, like an elaborate curriculum resource or a data management system. A large percentage (47 of 69, or 68%) turned out to be complex tools. Despite this, most of the interviewees seemed relatively comfortable themselves participating in this vast marketplace, though we occasionally caught glimpses of other kinds of discomfort. One teacher, for example, expressed exasperation with the lack of expertise on the part of people who shopped on her behalf, particularly as the Bloomberg culture wore off and the de Blasio culture took hold, and community school district superintendents and consultants gained more prominence:

> It is sort of an overwhelming feeling of disregard—not from the administration [of the school], but very much from the system. I think there's a lot of people making decisions [relative to investments in materials, technologies, curricula, and so on] that aren't in the classroom and aren't in touch, and they're just sort of these arbitrary, like "this sounds like a good idea, let's do this." And nobody is sort of conferenced with to say, "Well actually, that can't actually work in a classroom, or that doesn't include bilinguals, that doesn't include special needs."

In the New Direction that follows this chapter, we deal with how schools as communities of practice might acquire more information and more leverage in the marketplace of data use in teaching.

DATA USE AND POVERTY IN NEW YORK CITY

In this next stop on an exploration of the journey that the innovation we call data use in teaching has travelled (from the perspective of the schools we studied), we highlight a key objective of the innovation: the amelioration of poverty's impact on learning.

Utilization of Pupil Personnel Teams

Later in this section is the transcript of a Pupil Personnel Team (PPT) meeting in what is likely the most poverty-impacted school in our set of poverty-impacted schools. PPT meetings are a fixture in New York City schooling—as, indeed in many other cities and states under this or other names. Associated with special education policy, the team is multidisciplinary and tracks a wide range of student needs (academic, social, behavioral, medical, and psychological) and their effects on learning. A PPT tries to match needs with available resources. In this particular school, it functions as a bulwark against the intrusions of poverty, and it meets weekly. It is a good example of what we have described in another publication as a *policy adjustment in practice*—in this case, involving an adaptation of the special education referral process to make it do much more (Isacoff, Karin, & McDonald, 2018). In this school, as again in many others, the PPT is among the school's key users of data, and its conversations and actions can deeply affect teaching. This is because in a poverty-impacted school, poverty and any efforts to fight it play a role in nearly all teaching.

Acting within tight confines of space, time, resources, and context, team members portrayed in the transcript below are clearly coordinating their efforts, examining data of various kinds, stretching available resources, expanding their conception of what schooling is, and acting to ameliorate the impact of poverty on their students' lives. To put their efforts in proper context, we preface the transcript with an account of this middle school's larger relationship with poverty.

In U.S. schooling, poverty is defined on the basis of free and reduced-price lunch counts. The standard of eligibility for free lunch during 2013–2014, when this meeting occurred, was an annual gross income for a household of four of under $30,615. This school had a free lunch count then of 87%. However, most families whose children attended the school then subsisted on much less than $30,615. The city, using broader metrics, estimated that 30% of the families in the neighborhood where the school is located earned less than $24,300 (for a household of four)—making this slightly gentrifying neighborhood only the 12th poorest in New York City. However, the school draws its students mostly from the public housing that surrounds it, and thus substantially from this 30%. Moreover, while the bigger neighborhood would unlikely qualify for "truly disadvantaged" status in, for example, Chicago terms (where poverty can be deeper and neighborhood conditions far worse), it does present high levels of toxic risk (Wilson, 2012). For example, the neighborhood ranks 5th in the city on incarceration, 4th on community violence, 3rd on alcohol-related hospitalizations, 2nd on drug-related hospitalizations, and 1st on psychiatric hospitalizations (NYC Community Health Profiles, 2015).

Inside a PPT

The meeting begins promptly at 10 A.M. in a small conference area—squeezed into the principal's office, and separated from his desk by a half-wall. The pace of the meeting is brisk, encouraged by an occasional ding from the assistant principal's timer, and also by his facilitation. The briskness signifies urgency rather than either stress or ennui. The school alternates the focus of PPT meetings between boys and girls. Today is girls' day. The protocol is to begin with a quick academic update on each student to be discussed (from a list of students drawn up in advance by the principal, assistant principal, data coach, and counselor). The tone of the meeting is serious, but there is also levity at points, presumably to lighten the emotional load of this work. Instead of identifying participants by their pseudonym initial here (as in most of the rest of the book), we identify them by their roles in the school to emphasize the collaboration involved.

> *Assistant principal:* OK, Amelia.
> *Data coach:* She failed everything: humanities, math, science, and AfterSchool [a mandatory academic and recreational program]. She is very difficult to deal with, very surly with everyone. There was not one class this marking period where she found a safety net.
> *Principal:* This is a kid in crisis.
> *Social worker:* Definitely needs counseling—more like outside counseling than school-based counseling.
> *Assistant principal:* Maybe instead of *surly*, we have to think *depressed*. The foster mom seems to be in her 60s—no, she's more like 70.
> *Principal:* But there is a biological parent somewhere in the picture.
> *Counselor:* Yes, her mother is in a hospital with a chronic disease. She has foster siblings [that is, biological siblings who are in foster care elsewhere].
> *Data coach:* But *she's* not in foster care.
> *Principal:* Right, not official foster care.
> *Assistant principal:* Amelia is the daughter of her [unofficial foster mother's] best friend's daughter.
> *Principal:* Last night we did the student-led family conferences [a major innovation in the school in which the student assembles relevant data about their progress, and leads the reporting to their family], and I'd

like to see Amelia do it today with whoever shows up [for the make-up session for families who could not attend the evening before].

Assistant principal: Can we push outside counseling? Beth [AfterSchool program counselor] met with her [Amelia]. Is she [Beth] following up?

Data coach: She was a bitch to Beth. [Catches herself, and team members laugh]

Assistant principal: You mean the child was not warming up to her? [More laughter] Yeah, she's had several encounters like this.

A consensus is reached: The AP will push for a meeting between the caregiver and the outside counseling center—one that the school regularly works with.

Assistant Principal: Next, Starlight. Mom came last night. She's well under 30, not so far from her daughter's age.

Data coach: Star is failing nearly every class. But she came almost on time today. I asked her mom recently when I ran into her at the Discount Mart [a department store near the school, recently opened and one of the few retail outlets for clothes available for miles] to help us out with the uniform thing, but Star came today with half a thigh exposed. I decided not to press the issue. But I brought up the issue of her going to AfterSchool again starting next Monday—but do I believe this is going to happen?

At this point, a conversation ensues about the peer relationships among Amelia, Starlight, and Jacey (also a 7th-grade girl). The girls are close, though the consensus of these adults is that Amelia and Starlight are bad influences on each other, while Jacey is a good influence on both. The team members seem to have studied the relationship—perhaps across multiple PPT girls' meetings.

Data coach: Amelia is on the fence. Who knows what would happen if Jacey were not in her life? The three of them meet together in the girls' room [smiles around the table].

Teacher: But do you see that as a solution? [Data coach shakes her head no.] We could bring this up at the 7th-grade team meeting to plan steps.

Assistant principal: OK, Neesha.

Data coach: She's failing science and AfterSchool, but she is passing humanities and math. [Several team members nod or speak approvingly in response to the latter comment.]

Principal: The auntie who showed up last night [for the family conference] was vicious. I heard her speak to Neesha—very loud and ugly, and in the hallway. But we agreed at the conference on a conduct sheet—one that Neesha will carry from class to class to get teachers' daily OKs on her behavior, but the family has to monitor this, I said. We can't be responsible for ensuring that this happens every day. There's too much going on for us to monitor this dependably. Recently, Neesha asked if she could leave class to be available for a phone call from her father who is incarcerated. And I know that if you're incarcerated, you can't call just any time, so she sat in my office with her cellphone, and Dad did call. Then she came out of the call crying. Neesha can be so incredibly unpleasant, but when I heard the aunt talk to her—so ugly.

Counselor: Did she talk back?

Principal: No, she just took it.

Assistant principal: This is out of the protocol, but Julio Hernandez needs a winter coat. I know because I saw him today [subfreezing temperature outside] in just his hoodie. That's always the sign. And all the coats at the free store [part of the family conference last night] were taken. Almost everything got taken [including foodstuffs].

Dean (of discipline): Is he in a shelter?

Assistant principal: No

Dean: Well, I could see if I can get a coat for him at [names a nearby settlement house].

Data coach: No need, I have money I can use for that. Can you cover lunch for me, and I can run to Discount Mart to buy the coat?

Dean: Sure.

Assistant principal: OK, Tabiah.

Principal: There is a custody battle going on. Grandma and Grandpa from the south once had custody, and want it back. They think she will be less under bad influences there.

Counselor: I don't believe that, by the way.

Social worker: At least it's warmer there [laughter].

Assistant principal: It's 10:44, but we have two runaways that we have to talk about—Atarah and Charity. And we have to deal with grief counseling for several kids.

They make an arrangement for a subteam meeting, and the PPT meeting adjourns.

We think this is an extraordinarily revealing meeting—though likely one unimagined by many champions of data use in teaching. First, of course, there is the implicit depiction of poverty as a force that can easily crush learning, hope, and life, absent resilience, and people in a position to help foster resilience. Second, there is the tough-mindedness of this team—a key element of effective teaching in general, of data use in teaching in particular, and of resilience building. The participants start with the academic data because they understand that this is their responsibility to improve, but they move quickly to social or psychological rather than academic interventions because they also understand that these are likely to be more powerful in the cases they are exploring. In another session, however, they might very well have discussed such interventions as one-on-one reading support, additional after-school tutoring, or a switch from one classroom to another. Third, there is the team's vivid illumination of an attitude that we think is rare in school achievement emergencies, but much needed. It combines caring, rationality, pragmatism, and humor. Fourth, there is the energy displayed here in what in other schools can be a fairly mundane organizational routine, or a depressing and enervating one. These participants clearly draw on the diverse expertise of the group's members, and they put a premium on action now.

Meanwhile, the transcript reveals something about deep poverty and its impact in New York City that is important to note (for example) in contrast to poverty in rural Tennessee, or even suburban New York. The big city has resources that are rarely found elsewhere. So there is an after-school program in this school, and it provides counseling services. There is also an outside counseling center that the school can call on. There is a nearby settlement house. And although these are not mentioned at this meeting, there are also nearby hospitals and urgent care clinics, and family social work services.

A TEACHER'S VOICE

In advising researchers to study data use in practice across the complexities of the educational system, Judith Warren Little (2012) suggests alternating "zooming out" and "zooming in." We follow this advice throughout the book. In this chapter, we zoomed way out first, to federal and district policy, and the impact of a bustling marketplace. Then we zoomed in to look at poverty as educators encounter it in a New York City middle school. Next, we zoom still more closely in—to a 7th-grade teacher negotiating on a daily basis the experience of data use in teaching on her practice, and reflecting on more than a decade of influence of the innovation on her school's collective practice.

The teacher is Lorena Garcia (LG), and the interviewer Dana Karin (DK). DK has just observed a running record—a teacher-administered standardized reading assessment of a single student, meant to determine in part the student's reading level in terms of text complexity (from A to Z). The school uses the Teachers College Reading and Writing Project Running Record protocol, an intimate standardized assessment of miscues and comprehension challenges. In her opening question, DK refers to the text that LG has chosen for the running record, which is supposed to be at the student's current reading level. In her answer, LG suggests simply and plainly the role of intuition in teaching as partner to data use. It is an important point, and often overlooked by data use enthusiasts who imagine that data use is something more independent and precise—even magical.

DK: How do you know in the moment [of selection] that a student has moved up a level?

LG: We have an Excel sheet of where they were tested in June of last year, then we tested them in September and we have that in the sheet. So, I'm just referring back to the last level I tested them at and then I sort of guess. Do I think that they moved up a level? Do I think they moved up two?

DK: Do the results all go directly into the spreadsheet?

LG: Yes, into the spreadsheet, and I put the carbon copy of their actual running record [miscue analysis, and so on] into the binder.

Then LG acknowledges a vulnerability in the school's running records with respect to reliability (a dimension of validity), and she explains how she and her colleagues have addressed the problem. Her explanation portrays a faculty not simply dependent on their external literacy consultants at TCRWP, but rather invested themselves in identifying validity threats and addressing them.

Something that we talked about as a department in the beginning of the year is how we, as a team, do the running records because we did find that there was some disconnect in how we did it. Some teachers were giving kids passages and if the kid missed three words in the passage, they took them away and gave them a lower-level text [the TCRWP rule of how to proceed]. And then there were some teachers who were pushing kids to do passages that they couldn't. And so we figured, okay, how are we actually going to do this? How are we going to have, you know, a grade standard, a literacy team-wide standard for how we conduct a running record? So that a level X is a level X for anyone in the school. We worked a lot on that.

LG goes on to describe the impact of this assessment on students, and her remark richly illustrates one of the dynamics of teaching we explored in Chapter 2, the dependence of the teacher's efficacy on the student's cooperation (Cohen, 2011).

LG: A lot of the time, the kids get really nervous during the running record. They think that something very bad is going to happen. But it is also really helpful because it gives me like one-on-one, really nice one-on-one time with kids, where you force yourself to sit down and sometimes they give you a piece of information in that one-on-one time that is so helpful and just. . .[pause]. They feel attended to, and sometimes this makes them do so much better. And it's a nice confidence boost [for me] because so far, every kid that I've tested has moved up at least one level and most have moved up two.

DK: How far back do you track running records?

LG: I have their 6th grade ones, their end-of-6th grade, fall, January, and then this one.

DK: How do you use this record?

LG: A few ways, but I think, honestly, the most important one is to show the students the physical proof that they have grown as a reader, or *not* grown as a reader. So, it's a concrete, measurable way to say, "Look at all of the work that you've done, look at this, look at where you started, at where you are now." And I've seen kids get so emotional about their running record that they start crying. They want to call their mom, they want to call their dad, they want me to email, they just feel so proud of themselves because they can actually see, "Oh my God, I actually jumped in my reading level."

LG does a full class set of running records (averaging, as she told DK, 15 minutes per record) three times a year. While she conducts these assessments, the 27 (of 30) students not assessed that period read independently. Of course, orchestrating this independent reading, to ensure that every student is appropriately matched with a text and appropriately attentive to it for 45 minutes, is a major challenge. And LG acknowledged this challenge. Then, in the following comment, she acknowledged a deeper one. It inheres in teaching generally, though the innovation we trace in this chapter does not typically address it.

DK: What other challenges do you face?

LG: Not knowing how to access everybody. Not knowing how to meet every learner exactly where they're at. Not being able to figure out exactly what it is that a kid is passionate enough about to sort of hook them in.

Here we see that the innovation we've tracked in this chapter has landed squarely in Lorena Garcia's 7th-grade classroom. And we can discern from her account some of the impact of the landing.

LG now spends a good deal of her teaching time in one-on-one reading assessments. These are highly scripted by the vendor that provides the protocol and analyzes the data, but they do also allow her a significant amount of discretion. And LG likes the time and the intimate connection with her students that they also afford. We can infer from what she has to say that her students do too.

On the other hand, she remains responsible for organizing what 29 other students are doing in her classroom while she spends 15 minutes per pull (times 30, times 3 per year). This is not a simple planning task for a teacher like LG who refuses to consign her students' available learning time to (say) test-prep worksheets, or what teachers have long called "busywork" (by way of acknowledging that not all the work they assign is learning work). But the innovation we are tracking here implicitly insists that all work *must be* learning work. So, in large part, she devotes this available learning time to independent reading. This does not mean, however, that she allows students to browse at will among the substantial offerings of her classroom library, and "just" read. Instead, she has to ensure that they are reading at a level that will stretch them. And to ensure that this happens, she must somehow (1) make sure that she herself has read and remembers every single text (out of hundreds available); and (2) monitor and record what her students choose to read, and how assiduously, and with what enjoyment and understanding. Moreover, she needs to have back-up plans ready for students she knows are unlikely to be able to read independently for 45 minutes, or who might more productively spend this available learning time (for whatever reason) doing something else.

One complication of the role of *pulling* (see Chapter 2) as a prominent teaching behavior and assessment method is that teachers like LG have had to rethink what planning is. They need more than ever before to be able to plan together with colleagues, to share feedback on the plans they use, and to share with each other the time-consuming task of searching for good materials, ones that engage students with rich and well-scaffolded content. They have to think of planning less in terms of whole-period lesson plans focused on activities they personally lead, and more in terms of regular routines that allow them to teach in small groups or one on one while students work or read in relatively independent fashion.

Finally, we learn from this interview another impact of the innovation landing in LG's classroom. This is evident in the haunting way LG ends the interview—with a straightforward acknowledgment of what every experienced teacher knows (whether striving to teach in data-rich ways as LG does, or not), but that many nonteachers do not know (including ones who champion data use in teaching). This is that the connection between teaching and learning is never surefire, and therefore that using data to guide teaching (like using intuition to guide teaching) will always involve some slippage.

SUMMING UP

In this chapter, we have addressed the basic question: What is data use in teaching? It is an innovation on a long journey, one that started in a mid-20th-century Congressional hearing room, but has by now proceeded through multiple levels of policymaking that have transformed it. A constant on the journey has been a U.S. context rife with poverty among children, and typically insistent that schooling can be enough to cure it. To see the actual consequences of this poverty on learning, teaching, and schooling, we listened in on a weekly team meeting in a poverty-impacted school and neighborhood. We also explored a second constant on the journey—namely a marketplace full of resources more or less useful in managing the innovation in practice. In the New Direction that follows, we have more to say about interacting with this marketplace. Finally, we ended the chapter close to practice itself, in the company of a teacher who explains to us this innovation as she lives with it daily.

Curating the Material World

To curate is to select, organize, and oversee a focused collection drawn from a larger source. In education, the word is sometimes used to refer to the task that every teacher faces at every level of teaching from preschool to graduate school—namely to select, organize, and oversee material that they draw for teaching from all possible sources, including the Internet. But as we came to understand in our study, schools can be curators too. Indeed, two of the nine schools we studied were skillful curators. In what follows, we explore—via Q & A—the transfer of this word *curating* from the practices of museums to the practices of schools.

Should Schools Have Designated Curators?

We think that schools definitely need some means of curating beyond the curating their districts may supply, and to supplement the curating that individual teachers can manage. Having a designated curator, however, is probably a bad idea. Curating needs to be distributed, and multiple teachers need to be involved. One reason is that curating is not just about using knowledge, but about gaining it—and the more teachers who gain "material" knowledge, the better. The two curating schools we studied were team-based in their governance, and their curating (though they didn't use this word) was woven into the teamwork. Administrators in various roles kept an eye on schoolwide priorities and budget integrity, but the teams wielded most of the actual interaction with the marketplace. This seems to us a promising approach.

What Does School-Level, Team-Based Curating Involve?

There's no one recipe for curating educational material. But one element is *market monitoring*:

- What's available out there?
- How might it help us manage or solve problems we've identified?
- How much might a particular product cost—not just in dollars, but in time, training, habit-shifting, and so on?
- What do the reviews of the product have to say?
- Can we visit some school nearby that uses it?

A related element involves figuring out the *provenance* of the product:

- Where does this product come from?
- Does it really have a research base?
- Does it work as advertised?

A third element involves the product's potential *integration* with other parts of the collection:

- Who will own this product initially, try it out, show the rest of us how it works, figure out the changes it introduces into our ordinary teaching routines?
- If it works well on a pilot basis, who will help scale it up or determine that it is useful only in the primary grades, or in math, not science?

And, of course, an important element involves *oversight* of use once a product has been established; that is:

- How does the use of the product evolve?
- What innovations in practice spring from it?
- What difference does it make in student learning (and how do we know)?

What Role Should Districts Play in Curating?

Of course, curating the materials relevant to data use in teaching does and should operate at multiple levels, and in our research, we have seen its power and relative effectiveness at the state and district levels (for example, in the support of certain literacy curricula over others). But in the massive district we studied, curating at these "higher" levels may not be effective, like when the district discovered that the curating function of its data management system, ARIS, found few users (Siman et al., 2014). And central-office curating can even be dangerous, as the Bloomberg-Klein administration discovered when it briefly mandated certain literacy and math curricula citywide, in the process, threatening effective curating at lower levels of the system, and installing poorly understood curricula in many schools (McDonald, 2014). As for the schools in our study, all enjoyed great discretion in curating, though they made some mistakes. However, we understand from our meetings with Spencer colleagues (who studied smaller districts that gave schools little curating discretion) that these districts made mistakes too. And the schools' lack of control sometimes left school-based educators feeling disempowered.

PART II

DEEP DIVES INTO
DATA USE IN ACTION

CHAPTER 4

Complicated Plumbing at the Heights

In a 4th-grade classroom at Heights Elementary School in New York City, serving one of the city's most poverty-impacted neighborhoods, an interactive whiteboard stands near a teacher's desk. The whiteboard may signify for parents who visit that their children's school has not after all been left behind, that it has managed to shift from 19th- and 20th-century technologies in teaching to 21st-century ones—from chalk and blackboard to digital input and display. This morning, the whiteboard displays for members of our research team a color-coded spreadsheet, featuring students' scores on last spring's state language arts test, the fall's benchmark test, the winter's running records, and more. The display signifies for us that data is a preoccupation here, as indeed it is. But the shift to effective data use in teaching, as we came to learn, was still a work in progress—work we explore in this first of our four deep dives into data use in teaching.

SPREADSHEET AFTER SPREADSHEET

The principal at Heights, Anna Jones (AJ), has moved aggressively toward what she calls "data-driven instruction," and she told one member of our team, Nora Isacoff (NI), that she and the school's data coach, as well as grade-level teacher leaders, had created spreadsheet after color-coded spreadsheet on everything from state test records, to teacher-administered assessments, to a register of how often parents visit the school. They had done this data depiction, she said, because they believed that the school itself, the principal's job, and the teachers' jobs were all at risk, absent signs of overall growth in the school's standardized test scores. And they did it also because they knew that students themselves would be seriously at risk if they emerged from this school as challenged in literacy as they had been when they entered. They believed that focusing on data would help their students progress faster.

For some students here, the literacy challenge they face reflects their status as still emerging speakers of English, though sufficiently advanced by federal and state guidelines to be tested only in English. Some of these students have experienced disruptions in their previous schooling for reasons that range from war to periods of homelessness to changes in their foster family assignments. All the students are challenged by poverty. The principal encourages teachers to share the spreadsheets with their students on a regular basis, explaining—to our skeptical ears—that "looking at data where students can compare themselves to the whole group really motivates them. They can see that some of them are at 30%. Some of them aren't even at 10%, and now they know where to go next."

AJ designed the Heights system of data use in teaching, and proudly describes it for NI as if it were a marvel:

> Just that one system connects to the administration, it connects to the classroom, it has the teacher support. Then it goes to student and family, because the family gets your rubric and all of that. You have your anecdotals, report card, and all of that. And then it would go up to the information, which all of this connects to. And then also other informational pieces, which we have there, which would be the attendance. We can look there and at tests. We can look at previous report cards and records of students. So, there it is, where this system kind of sums everything up.

Asked to articulate the system's underlying rationale—its theory of action—the school's data coach, Olive London [OL], speaks in a more distant voice, enumerates plausible steps, but ends magically:

> I believe that the underlying assumption is, if you assess students properly, and you analyze the results, and you analyze where the children are struggling and where the students are weak, then you'll be able to then meet higher demands.

Both professionals' accounts of the system ignore a lot of complicated plumbing—with joints, for example, between content knowledge and assessment, between test results and analysis of them, between discerning a student's struggle and knowing how to deal with it effectively, between teachers' higher demands and students' willingness to meet them, between students' encounters with their own performance data and their motivation to improve. Any of these joints can and will leak, even break. So it always goes with a theory of action. Still, a school cannot progress in the circumstances that Heights Elementary School faces without a theory of action—that is, without an articulated, intentional plan that identifies action steps, joints, and expected outcomes (Argyris & Schön, 1996). But even *with* a theory of action in place, there is still always the question: Who will mind the plumbing? Who will inspect for leaks? Who will fix breaks, or reroute pipes as needed? If students scoring in the red zone on the spreadsheets (the bottom of four performance bands on the state test) are disheartened rather than inspired by the plain talk about their status, how will they be rescued? For example, there is Trevor who, in response to his teacher's prompt, told one member of our research team that he is coded entirely red. "I have a hard time reading," he explained in a sad voice. Trevor may not resist his teacher's help as overtly as children in less well-behaved 4th-grade classrooms might, but he may resist nonetheless—quietly, with silence, a vacant stare, a dropped head. And even higher achieving students may resist, as OL suggests:

> You know students can sit; they can do the task; they can answer questions. But are they really participating at the deep-thinking level? How do you know the kids are solving the problems? As opposed to, say, the teacher laying out all the steps, and there's not really a lot of deep thinking on the part of the kids.

Meanwhile, teachers "who lay out all the steps" may resist OL's coaching. They too may think that their students are *unable*. Or they may feel harassed by spreadsheets. Even teachers like our focal teacher, Fiona Robb (FR), may lack sufficiently honed knowledge of how literacy develops to infer alternative moves from data displays alone. And even skillful help from coaches like OL may not be enough to help them monitor and address the range and depth of the learning needs their students face. More fundamentally, though less obviously, the literacy assessments available to FR and her colleagues, the same ones that yield all these data displays, may imperfectly align with the actual practices of literacy, and with the contours of learning these practices.

One of the teachers we interviewed at another school had a strategy for dealing with this predictable problem. "It's not just that I give them the test and call it a day," he said. "I'll give them several different assessments, and have them read aloud to me. I'll look at what they're doing in class, look at the books they've chosen. So much more data than people think there is." To identify and collect this other data, and to make sense of it, however, one must be deeply knowledgeable about literacy and how it develops, and one must also be aware that every assessment merely samples the larger domain; it does not map the domain in fine detail.

FR may think that all her student Trevor needs to improve his reading are worksheets focused on specific subskills identified by the state assessments, and "regrouping" with peers working on the same subskills. Indeed, as it turns out, these two instructional moves—worksheets and regrouping, alone or in combination—dominated all the 4th-grade classrooms we observed in this study. This is likely because both moves seem suited to the complexity of the situations teachers face in schools like Heights—for example, Trevor's need to regain lost time and opportunity to learn specific skills he has somehow failed to master, and FR's need to deploy her teaching across so many different patterns of similarly missed mastery. But the apparent suitability is illusory. Of course, underskilled students like Trevor need skills-focused work, but worksheets, whether worked on alone or in so-called same-skill peer groups, are insufficient, and in massive doses counterproductive. This is because they typically do only what most are intended to do, namely drill down.

However, learners like Trevor need lots of macrolevel work too: composing and deciphering bigger chunks of text. And they need to do much of this in the company of higher-skilled peers in order to gain a sense of where they themselves might aim and of what the process of reading in the real world looks like and sounds like. And they also need the intense company of an adult coach with deep expertise. Trevor may need skillful one-on-one help in decoding—maybe 15 minutes a day for some period of days, until he reaches an "aha!" moment of fluency, and in the process, gains a sense that he is not doomed to stay indefinitely red (Neuman, 2016).

There are systems of instruction—curricula—that encourage rich toggling between micro- and macrolevels of literacy teaching. These can work well when teachers work together to make the toggling serve students' needs, and when they do not treat particular literacy programs as plug-in curricula (to be simply installed and followed). At Heights, however, the focus on data seems to crowd out thoughtful attention to curriculum.

OBSERVATION OF A LESSON

As our team member Susan Neuman (SN) begins her observation, all the 4th graders are at their desks with a workbook. FR is the teacher. There is also an assistant teacher present. SN later learns that the data coach, Olivia London (OL), recommended the focus for this lesson—namely sequencing—based on her item analysis of last spring's 4th-grade New York State ELA test. FR explains to the class:

> Today we are going to be working on sequencing. We're going to be working on the words: *finally*, *first*, *then*, and *last* on pages 59–60. If you see one of the sequence words, underline it.

As the assistant teacher roams among desks, and helps children follow, FR reads from the designated pages, scrolling through them on the whiteboard, and pausing to ask questions. "What figures of language do we see here?" "What do we mean by *endangered*?" Sometimes a child answers, sometimes not. Among the children, there is a lot of slouching, and wandering eyes.

FR: Do you hear any signal words?

S: After.

FR: That's right [and she rereads the sentence in which the word *after* is located].

FR: Can anyone else find a signal word? [A student raises her hand.]

FR: [Calling on the student] Locate it in the text and read the sentence [Student complies. The word is *first.*]

FR: What does that word signal? [Child answers.]

FR: [Repeating what the child has said] Yes, that means where to begin.

The reading, punctuated by questions and answers, takes about 15 minutes. The attention is focused on the "signal" words, or ones that signal sequence, rather than on the science content of the passage.

Following the read-aloud, however, students are told to complete a worksheet that does deal with science content. As the students work on their worksheets, FR walks among them with a clipboard. She says to one student, "I love how you go back into the text to get the answer." She asks another student, "What is a *hypothesis*?"—a word referenced in the worksheet. The child answers: "An educated guess," and FR replies, "Very nice." And she asks another, "What step did Sam follow to prove his hypothesis? What step did he take in his experiment?" This is again a reference to the text. The child answers by putting his head on his desk. FR makes a note on her clipboard.

Meanwhile, as other students continue their worksheet work, the teacher and assistant teacher convene two guided reading groups (small groups reading in turn a single leveled text, with teacher guidance). FR sits in a circle with her guided reading group, and each child reads orally in turn from a nonfiction text. When a student stumbles, FR tries to help the student by sounding out the beginning sound, or pointing out the root word. But the students themselves exhibit no strategies on their own. Meanwhile, their posture suggests disengagement: slouching, looking in other directions, apparent drowsiness. The guided reading group ends without comprehension discussions or conversations. Then all the children line up to go to lunch, after completing an exit slip, answering the question, "How does analyzing a sequence of events help our understanding of the text?"

TEACHING IN CENTERS

In the interview excerpt below, one of the Heights Elementary School's grade-team leaders describes the kind of teaching and learning environment she and her colleagues are working to establish in the 4th grade. It is quite different from the environment most 4th-graders experience today in the U.S., and have for decades. However, it has both contemporary counterparts, test-focused and behaviorally strict urban charter schools (Green, 2015; Merseth et al., 2009), and also historical counterparts, the efficiency-focused urban "platoon" schools of the early 20th century (Tyack, 1974).

At the start of the interview, NI asks the team leader, Alena Martinez (AM), how data informs her instruction, and AM immediately shows the researcher her data binder.

> *AM:* (referring to the data binder.) The kids took a test online. After they took the test, I looked at it and analyzed which standard each question hits, and projected maybe why they got that question wrong. And then I created a 6-week plan for small groups, and what standards to hit depending on how many students got that wrong. So, this [showing binder page] was each question—who got it correct and who got it wrong and the percentage of kids in each 4th-grade class, compared to school-wide data.
>
> *NI:* So how exactly do you use this?
>
> *AM:* Well, in terms of math, after a test, we see which standards the kids did not master, and we'll do, like a little reteach for a week to see if they need like intensive work in those certain areas. And also depending on looking ahead, we'll look at skills that are worked on within the unit and focus more on them from a pretest point of view to see what skills we should focus more on—like lessons and creating centers around those.
>
> *NI:* So, you change what you teach based on. . .
>
> *AM:* Data. We do pretest and posttest, and then if they still didn't master the posttest, we also create reteach tests and have a week of centers and reteaching focusing on the standards that the kids missed. [By "centers," AM means interventions that may last several weeks, and straddle the classroom and after-school tutoring]. So, we always differentiate all our lessons.

Of course, deep content knowledge by teachers is always crucial in helping students understand, but it is particularly important in managing the process that AM describes, involving a sequence of teach/test/reteach/ retest where the online vendor is only doing the testing, not the teaching. In her account, AM infers from the original test items "the standards that the kids missed." But even if the test vendor had identified these standards for her, she and her team would still need to design the reteaching themselves. Yet what can easily happen under these circumstances—given constraints on teachers' content knowledge, or time, or both—is that the designers may focus too narrowly on the test items students got wrong, and orient the re-teaching around new items that mimic these. This is classic "teaching to the test," and it creates a leak in the plumbing. A test item is only a construct meant *to sample* the standard. It is not the standard itself. To "reteach" to it is to spill uselessly a lot of instructional time. The process AM describes can just keep kids in the red (Neuman, 2016).

> *NI:* You talked about one kind of data—standardized test data. Is there any other kind of data that you think of as informing your team's instruction?
>
> *AM:* Well, even just little exit slips or even checks for understanding. Throughout the lesson, I'll always say "thumbs up if you understand it, thumbs down if you don't, thumbs sideways if you need a little bit more help." And the kids do two problems, and if they get them both correct, they get a green card. And they have certain problems that they'll do on the computers, whereas the other groups—the red and the orange cards—they'll get pulled for an immediate reteach, and we have different activities for those groups also.
>
> *NI:* Have you always used data in this way, or is this something that's new?
>
> *AM:* It's kind of new, just because, you know, I didn't really understand it at first. And then I went to a workshop, and I'm still adjusting to it and trying to find new ways to use it. It's a lot of work.

THE DATA COACH

In our interview of data coach Olive London, she revealed the role that she plays in the creation of what AM called "centers," though OL used the term "small grouping," and her references to it went beyond skills-based groups to include interest-based and project-based ones.

> We do things like small grouping. Not small group as in the same classroom, but we've done things like separated the students across a grade, based on a particular skill or topic that we're interested in or trying to pursue, language sometimes, or if the students need more visuals, have special needs, you know, those that are more musical, maybe create their own rap to memorize something or whatever. Trying to find those different little niches that they have. Trying to get students to group themselves sometimes. That's one of the other areas that—for higher levels, you want the students to begin to manage themselves and take ownership of their own learning, so we use the assessments with the kids and say, "Okay, you did this. What do you think you could do next?" A different setting or project-based or a particular topic—if they can handle it. I mean, it depends where they are. But, a lot of [what I do] is for instruction. Instruction and grouping are the two main things. And so, we're doing all this collection. We look at all this data. We review all this data. We try to make plans based on the data. But it's not converting to increased test scores. So that's where our challenge as a school is.

At this point in the interview, OL zeros in on another kind of data, and she turns out to be among the small number of participants in our study—as noted in Chapter 1—who indicated interest in data regarding misconceptions.

> *OL:* We have to get better at the ongoing, in-the-middle-of-the-lesson getting information on the kids and making adjustments. So, like, if a kid has a misconception, and I keep on going—this is a bad habit. We're trying to catch that—but at the same time, staying on target with the lesson and keeping everybody moving forward.
>
> *NI:* Do you think a teacher can do both of those things at once—stop to explore the misconception and also move forward?
>
> *OL:* I think a lot of it has to go with the planning before you do it, and the biggest issue is the time, because you have to—as you're looking at the lesson, you can look at data to tell you what you think the students know and what you think they need to learn, but you need to be able to look at the lesson you're going to teach and think, What are the possible misconceptions students might have here? And be prepared with a response when those come up.

Of course, this requires deep content knowledge on the teacher's part, and since this is elementary school, it is deep content knowledge across multiple content areas. OL does not underestimate the challenge.

> [This is] very challenging for a lot of teachers. Your best teachers struggle with it. Teachers that are *struggling teachers* are really struggling, like they're really having a hard time. But I think that's something that's been identified for our school as something we need to change, we need to work on. So, we're still looking to figure that out.

IS THERE A "WE" AT HEIGHTS?

The innovation we are exploring in this book is a disruptive one, and intended to be. That is, it means to change several formerly deep-grained habits of teaching—habits ranging from relying exclusively on teacher intuition instead of data collection and analysis, to the habit of expecting too little of students who may initially score poorly on tests. However, the thing about disruptive innovations is that they typically disrupt in ways that go beyond the foreseen. Olive London tracks the intended disruption that data use in teaching is creating in her school, and she works hard to steer her colleagues through it. She prepares spreadsheets for them so that they are not dependent wholly on their intuition and their previous experience in understanding their students' strengths and weaknesses; then she coaches them as they act on this information. In the process, however, she learns that the spreadsheet information is still insufficient, and she works to open their practices to another kind of data too—data from practice itself, from what Donald Schön (1983) calls reflection-in-action, and what she calls "middle-of-the-lesson getting information on the kids." So she coaches them to ponder potential misconceptions, and to pause when they spot one. "What do you mean, Trevor?" she hopes they'll learn to ask. "Say more." But she worries, as she told us, that the press for "one assessment after another assessment after another assessment"—referring not just to big-testing but to interim testing that mimics it, and to intimate standardized testing like one-on-one reading assessments—crowds out the possibility of such inquiry-based teaching. There is too little time and too much pressure to land on narrowly-defined "right" answers.

Meanwhile, there is another disruptive impact that OL fails to see clearly, and she is complicit in creating it. It has to do with the culture of central control in charge of the innovation, not just at federal, state, and district levels, but especially here in the school. She says, with regard to the issue of pausing and inquiring in the face of misconception, that "we" need to work on it and that "we're" looking to figure it out, but she misconstrues the strength of "we-ness" in this school. In fact, the spreadsheets—centrally devised by her and others in the administrative team—function as directives for teachers, not texts they are expected to discuss and puzzle over, or supplement with intimate data including samples of student work. Principal AJ told us that data has to be "displayed, discussed, and owned." The display part of this formulation is, of course, the spreadsheets. But the discussion part involves very little actual discussion. It takes the form largely of a supervisory meeting in which the principal (P) and an assistant principal (AP) quiz a teacher (T) and an assistant teacher (AT) on the spreadsheets and other artifacts of the innovation. We observed one such meeting, and we provide a brief excerpt below to illustrate the prosecutorial tone of it, one not well suited to fostering ownership. Here, as we did once before, we depart from our usual habit in the book of using initials to identify speakers. To emphasize the hierarchical dimension, we use roles instead:

> *P:* Remember last time you guys had some professional learning in your classrooms, we asked you to look at your lowest-third children, what you're doing for them. We're going to discuss all that and what your next steps are, not only for your lowest-third but for your upper-level kids so that we don't have any stagnating, any plateauing. So, let's go. We have James who is soaring but has plateaued. He came in quite higher than all the other children, so—what happened? is the question I would ask you.
>
> *T:* I didn't do his first [assessment]. Someone else tested him. And when I read with him, he read beautifully, but he couldn't remember the story.
>
> *AP:* So, the comprehension is not there, is that what you're saying?

T: His fluency is great. His comprehension, he can't remember. He remembered the ending detail, and then, that's it.

AP: So, what are you doing for him?

T: We've been working on story elements, the five elements: character, setting, beginning, middle, and end.

P: And is he doing any better?

T: He is.

P: And what about these other kids [pointing to a projected spreadsheet]?

T: They all moved up except James didn't.

P: Did you guys make any notes in your student summaries?

T: In the anecdotals.

P: Okay, so there's a lot on him, and that is where we get a full picture of a child, right?

T: Right. We gave him an individualized behavior chart. It seems to be working a little bit.

AT: His behavior is improving, but his academics are much lower than. . .

AP: Much lower than you originally thought?

AT: No, he was never thought to be. . . He's much lower in comparison to all of his peers in the classroom.

AP: So how come he doesn't have any data for his benchmark?

T: He does. If you go to F&P it's there [the reference is to a log associated with text complexity levels, as defined in an earlier edition of Fountas & Pinnell, 2016].

AP: But it's not in *here*, in the chart.

To cultivate teacher ownership of a disruptive innovation like data use in teaching, the champions of it have to operate in ways that suggest the presence of a community of inquiry, one capable of drawing on and considering multiple sources of data and intuition, one committed to collective action. Donald Schön described this as "a context in which something is at stake"—as it surely is at Heights Elementary School—"and our worry," as Schön continued, "is how to take action, with a sense that we *have* to take action, and that there is a *we* here that's trying to do this." He added that he found in such circumstances the "greatest grounds for hope" (quoted in Cervone, 2007, p. 160). We call this kind of context an *action space*, and we explore it in the next chapter's deep dive.

A TRUST LEAK

When asked what she regarded as the biggest challenge to her efforts to create a data-driven school, Principal AJ told us simply: "teachers." When asked to clarify, she said, "Eh, you know, teachers." When asked again what she meant, she said that for some teachers, data use becomes just "another thing to do." But, knowing how important it is, she told us, she "pushes them on it."

NI asked her whether the school might be overwhelmed by data. AJ answered quickly, "I wish I could get more," though then she paused to acknowledge a problem with the system she had proudly created and continued to tend closely.

> Yes, we have all of these things, but now we have to delve further. Because what we've noticed is that, yeah, we have it—it's there. But is it being really understood by teachers? Because what they're supposed to do is then take that data and look how this data will improve the curriculum and then look at what skills the kids are not getting, and that's when they go to the book, and they develop, and they use that as a guiding piece but not as the teaching piece.

Then, suddenly, AJ shifts her complaint.

AJ: And because of this, everybody, you know, is blaming me.
NI: What do you mean they're blaming you?
AJ: I made all this up [laughing]. They think I made it up [the press for data use in teaching]. They think I'm just doing it to be a bitch.
NI: Why *are* you doing it?
AJ: Because I find it very useful. It's really a dialogue to say, did you *see* this? A teacher will have the same lesson plan for two lessons, and you're saying, do you *get* it!? This is not about designing a lesson to make yourself look good. It all has to do with efficacy. But when we did the school survey . . . [New York City annually surveys teachers, parents, and in secondary schools, students, on elements that include issues of trust. Results are published on each school's website] . . . I did terribly. We usually do very well, but in the last 3 years, it started to drop—trust. We really had sucky trust issues. And when that happens, the first thing they do is blame me and the administration. It was psychological. Teachers have never been taught how to get over stuff, you know, being sensitive to stuff, how to open up to take criticism, to be able to see that we're in here as a team.

Indeed, AJ is likely not wrong about how Heights teachers perceive her leadership. One told us, "We're such a data-heavy school, and honestly, I think we spend way too much time on data." When NI asked the teacher why she thought there was so much attention to data at Heights, the teacher answered, "It's our principal. She's crazy with data." Then she went on to complain about the school's policy of devoting the first and last month of the year to assessment of students by teachers other than their own. This teacher said she thinks it reflects the principal's belief that "sometimes teachers cheat and write down false things to help their MOSL improvement [measurement of student learning metric, which figures into each teacher's evaluation]."

The good news is that the principal has spotted a leak. The bad news is that this school is not well equipped for fixing leaks.

SUMMING UP

In this first deep dive, we visit an elementary school whose principal articulates a strong but hyperrational—or magical—idea of data use in teaching. The principal shows up twice in the deep dive—first to explain her system of "pushing" for data use, and later to acknowledge a problem with it. She has discovered, as we put it, a trust leak. Indeed, there is too little "we" in this school, though the innovation it is trying to implement demands a "we." The principal's partner in pushing data use in teaching is an assistant principal/teaching coach, who also shows up twice in the deep dive, near the beginning where she offers a somewhat less magical account of the innovation than the principal offers, and near the end where she acknowledges the crucial role in teaching of inquiring on the spot. Yet the lesson we see on this dive shows little room for inquiring on the spot. It's a plodding lesson, though it is suggested by the assistant principal based on her analysis of test items on the last state standardized test, items that focused on "signal words." At the bottom of the deep dive, we also meet a boy named Trevor for whom the school's fixation on big-test data analysis and grouping and regrouping with color-coded cards is likely the wrong teaching strategy.

Distributing Leadership

Advancing the innovation called data use in teaching from theory into practice requires the distribution of leadership. This typically starts with an acknowledgment by principals, at least implicitly, that they cannot possibly direct the activities of all the people who report to them. Other means of direction are needed—including a strong guiding vision for the school, strong and positive norms for interaction, and operational teams (Spillane, 2006; Spillane & Diamond, 2007). Such teams might include, for example, one that interprets big-test data pouring in at the school level by the light of intimate data (from, for example, reading inventories and student writing samples); another that connects subject teachers with teaching specialists across grade levels, and school teachers with after-school teachers; and still another that curates the material world with the needs of the school's children in mind. Meanwhile, managing teams like these requires more than the two kinds of leadership typically associated with school leadership—namely managerial and instructional. It requires facilitative leadership too—the capacity to bring people together, and to help them learn together, act together, and reflect together on action (Bryk et al., 2010)

Of course, facilitative leadership incorporates some of the skills associated with leading classrooms full of children—for example, careful preparation and follow-up, promotion of inclusive participation, and deft management of problems on the spot. But it requires a shift of persona when the people led are colleagues rather than children. In their 2013 book, *The Power of Protocols,* Joseph McDonald, Nancy Mohr, Alan Dichter, and Elizabeth McDonald write that this other persona depends first of all on an "appointment"—that is, something in the school's "constitution" that lends the leader the "right" to plan an agenda, steer a group toward some goal, delegate responsibilities, and so on. This "constitution" might be the annual school leadership plan, the faculty's vision statement, the principal's cabinet blueprint, and so on. And the persona depends too on cultivating a skill set matched to the tasks. Facilitative leaders should be able to adopt believable neutrality, help others suspend their disbelief, and summarize diverse viewpoints fairly. In addition to just getting stuff done, they should view themselves as building collegial trust—not personal trust, but situational trust—the consequence over time of a group's norms and history (McDonald, Mohr, Dichter, & McDonald, 2013).

Besides the McDonald et al. (2013) book, we also recommend David Allen and Tina Blythe's (2004) book, *The Facilitator's Book of Questions*, and the website and professional development activities of the School Reform Initiative (SRI) (www.schoolreforminitiative.org). Allen and Blythe supply deeply insightful virtual coaching for facilitative leaders, and SRI provides an immensely diverse collection of formats they can try out on their own.

CHAPTER 5

Action Space at Bayside

Our second deep dive into data use in a school takes us to the deepest point first, where we explore the complex interactions among a single student, his teacher, and a text. We call this "space" a *wild triangle*, borrowing a metaphor from McDonald (1992). As suggested in Chapter 2, this is where teacher, student, and content intersect. After exploring the wildness there, we explore how this middle school has organized itself to deal with it, as well as with insistent calls from system higher-ups to use data in the process. We find that enterprising school leaders have reframed calls for data use in teaching into ground-level action teams. These draw on teachers' practical skills, on resources from a sprawling marketplace, on modest extra funding, and on community support.

DEEP DOWN

In school, everything ultimately depends on a recurring triangular relation-ship among a teacher, a student, and some object of their attention. The object may be a text, a concept, or a practice. People who have never taught, or never reflected deeply on their own moments of learning in classrooms, may assume that the points of this triangle are well defined, as in a triangle printed on paper. But it is much more useful to think of this triangle as a lightshow projected on a dance floor, with angles shifting continually. The shifts reflect changes in what the teacher and the student think and sense as they work together and apart, and also changes in the challenges and opportunities they perceive in what they are working on and with. Yet these incessant changes are merely one source of the "wildness" in the triangle. Another is relational predicaments always at hand—whether, for example, to take some risk or not, to go along or resist, to dig deeper or pass over (Cohen, 2011; Lampert, 2001; McDonald, 1992). And wildness oozes also from a thicket of contextual variables that include the teacher's funds of knowledge, the student's readiness to learn, and, of course, the influence of all the other wild triangles in the room. In any case, the triangle is where the innovation we explore in this book really aims, though most of the "aimers" (that is, the higher-up champions of the innovation) have little sense of its wildness. That is why we dive deep down first.

The particular triangle we sketch below is defined by an English teacher named Annmarie Smith (AS) who teaches at Bayside Middle School in New York City, a 7th-grade boy named Kahlil, and a rich text entitled *Lyddie*, Katherine Paterson's (1991) young-adult historical novel of mill life in New England. AS is a veteran teacher who at this moment in her career is both striving and struggling to fulfill massively heightened expectations of what she can achieve in her work with Kahlil and his classmates. These expectations are her own, as well as her colleagues' and community's. They derive from multiple policy sources beyond the school and community, and they have deeply affected both the school's organization and AS's teaching and her thinking about teaching. Meanwhile, Kahlil has difficulty decoding, and according to his teacher has unspecified "trouble" at home that he may nearly always be thinking about.

Then there are the 27 other 7th-graders in Kahlil's class (participating themselves in 27 uniquely wild triangles). More than half of these classmates either have, as Kahlil does, an individualized educational plan (IEP) meant to accommodate one or more specifically identified disabilities, or they are still emerging English speakers. Some bring both these circumstances to their respective learning.

Enveloping all the students and their teacher are the procedures, routines, and culture that have been built up in this classroom, and indeed across this school, and that AS and her students typically follow but occasionally disregard, and in either event negotiate. In what follows, we portray a single wild triangle within this classroom context—defined by Paterson's text, AS's teaching, and Kahlil's learning. The portrayal is drawn from the low-inference observation notes of researcher Joseph McDonald (JM), as enhanced later the same day by higher-inference details provided by AS. To enhance the intimacy of the portrayal, we maintain the first-person narration of these enhanced original notes.

Inside the Triangle

AS reads aloud the beginning four pages of *Lyddie*, chapter 9. The rest of the room, including me, reads silently after a boy (Kahlil) kindly offers me a book from the class bookcase. AS privately asked me to sit in the back, and to offer as needed a little support to the most challenged readers in the class who would be sitting near me. She told me that another visitor the previous day had done this to good effect. I agreed. One of the boys is Kahlil.

Following the read-aloud, AS engages the class in a "chaining" exercise that begins with private talk by "partners" and then proceeds to "table talk" about the question of what Lyddie feels in chapter 9 as she encounters the mill for the first time as a 13-year-old millworker. The desks are arranged to form "tables," seating four students in two-partner sets. To start off, AS asks us (I have become Kahlil's partner, given the absence of his usual one)

to refer to the portion of the novel that she has just read aloud, and to use
our "chapter notes" in considering this question. Completing the notes for
chapter 9 constituted the writing portion of the previous night's homework.
As his partner, I ask Kahlil to brainstorm with me "feelings" that the read-
aloud text seems to suggest. I encourage him, as AS did, to use his chapter
notes, but I see quickly when he pulls them out that they are quite rudimen-
tary and useless for this task. "Can you think of any Lyddie feelings you
remember from the reading?" I ask, and he deflects my question, turns his
head, smiles, shakes his head no, lowers his head, opens his book, and stares
at it. I persist, however, and eventually he comes up with "She feels stupid."
It occurs to me that Kahlil at this moment also feels stupid, but his reply
does have textual legitimacy: at one point in the text, the girl who teaches
Lyddie how to work the looms at the mill asks her if she likes to read, and
Lyddie responds that she has not had much schooling.

Given Kahlil's hesitations, we do not get to the table-level talk before
AS starts the chain. It is produced by one "volunteer" or "cold-called" student from each of the room's eight tables taking turns (AS told me in an
earlier interview that she always cold calls students who look like they are
hoping someone else will be called on). Whether volunteering or cold-called,
contributors to the chain must not only share aloud a feeling their table discussed, but incorporate it into what previous tables have said. In this man-
ner, the chain gradually becomes a long statement about Lyddie's feelings
on her first day at the mill, which Smith tracks on the whiteboard. She does
not, however, track it verbatim, which adds a memory challenge to the task,
as if the chain were a cumulative children's rhyme.

The cold-called student who speaks at table 1 offers "surprised," and
AS asks him to put that word into a full sentence. The boy answers, "When
Lyddie got into the mill, she was surprised by the noise." The next table
contributor says, "nervous," but AS asks him to add his table's response to
the previous table's response, and he answers, "When Lyddie got into the
mill, she was surprised by the noise. When she got into the mill, she was nervous." AS asks him to paraphrase the first table's response in adding on his
table's response, and he struggles. But she approves the following attempt:
"When Lyddie got into the mill, she was surprised and nervous about all the
noise." Then the next table contributor, after repeating this sentence, adds
a second: "She was happy to be making money for her family." AS quibbles
briefly with *happy* on interpretive grounds, but lets it stand.

Our table is fourth in the chain, and to help Kahlil if he is called upon
(as I suspect he may be), I whisper quietly as if for myself the other tables'
answers: "Okay, surprised, nervous, happy. . . ." Indeed, AS does call on
Kahlil, and he says "She feels stupid." Again, AS quibbles a little—as if
modeling interpretive thinking: "I'm not sure I'd say *stupid*, but maybe."
She ends up allowing the word, however, then presses Kahlil to recapitulate
the previous responses before adding his own in a complete sentence. He

does this haltingly but satisfactorily, and the chain moves on. By the end, our "chained" statement is elaborate, though more in its array of feelings than in its syntax. Nonetheless, a starter sentence—really a single word— has grown into an interpretive paragraph.

Meanwhile, Kahlil seems pleased with the part he has played in this success, and participates several times in the next exercise, which involves looking at the image of a large mechanical loom that AS projects. It is an image the students have seen and discussed previously in their social studies class (coordinated with English Language Arts at Bayside). This refresher seems to be support for their continued homework reading. AS asks for volunteers who will walk to the screen, point to an element of the loom, and name it. Kahlil comes up three times, walking jauntily, but each time he says nothing. On the third trip, however, he points to a part of the loom, looks at AS, and she supplies the name. And on his way back, she asks him to distribute Post-it pads to all the tables (apparently a job he is often assigned). While he gets the Post-it pads and begins the task, she explains that she wants the tables to record on these Post-its "textual evidence of the feelings" articulated in the chain, and to try to associate these with working conditions in the mill.

At this point, I'm paying more attention to how much Kahlil is enjoying his Post-it pad job than to AS's directions, but when he finishes the job, I do my best to fill him in. I edit out the part about working conditions, however. I simply say that we should look for evidence in the chapter to back up his argument that Lyddie feels stupid on her first day at the mill. As it turns out, Kahlil gets stuck on this first task anyway, and just stares at the book as I prod gently. Soon, AS asks for the Post-it notes to be turned in, but we have none to offer. Our table colleagues produce one or two, however, and this covers up for us.

Post-Observation Interview

Following the class, JM sat down with AS to debrief. Here is an excerpt from this interview:

> *JM:* I felt like I was one of your students today because I was Kahlil's partner.
> *AS:* I wish he was showing more progress.
> *JM:* But I thought he made some progress today, a little bit.
> *AS:* He makes a little bit every time. And he likes me now, so he is more willing to try. He was very combative with me at the beginning of the year—
> *JM:* Was he?
> *AS:* I would say one thing to him, and he would get very defensive and completely shut down. There's a lot of kids like him here: Elijah, who was in the front over there, and Isaiah.
> *JM:* Is Isaiah the kid who yelled out the window?

Here JM inadvertently draws AS toward another of the wild triangles, and she begins to speak more generally, using plural pronouns. Even when he tries twice to bring her back to Kahlil's triangle, he fails.

> *AS:* Yeah. They're acting out because they have a very low frustration level. They get off task because they don't want to feel this frustration. I understand all of that, but I don't let them get away with it. I try to make them feel as comfortable and respected as possible, but I try to guide them in various ways so that I do get something out of them.
>
> *JM:* What were you consciously thinking about Kahlil today as you taught him?
>
> *AS:* A general feeling I have with most kids is that I just don't want to walk away and have them not say anything, so that they feel like they can rely on someone else's thinking. They have to say something, take ownership of their learning.
>
> *JM:* Yes, you were pressing Kahlil.
>
> *AS:* I feel like I do it in a way that's friendly, and that I do genuinely want to hear from them. I try to get that feeling across to them, which I feel most of the time they get it. So, it's why they finally say something.

This is the ground that the innovation called data use in teaching aims for—where unique learners like Khalil, in crowds of roughly 30, organized by classroom routines and norms, work away, day after day. It is where teachers like AS may press them, as she does here, with a challenging text, cold calls, and follow-up questions. As she does this pressing, AS bears in mind particular needs and tactics for meeting them—ones etched on her teaching intuition by experience and data briefings. They may tell her, for example, that Khalil needs lots of assistance, and that she can persuade visitors to class to help supply it; and that at times he needs to walk freely around the room handing out supplies, and will signal her in some way that he needs this movement. Or they may tell her that Isaiah is prone to yell out the window or engage in other inappropriate classroom behavior in order to relieve flashes of frustration, but that she can deal with this quietly, while ensuring that all her other students remain calm and productive.

HIGHER UP IN THE BAYSIDE SYSTEM

A later interview of AS by JM begins with some complaints from her about the pressures she feels to use data in teaching, even as she is still adjusting to what "data use in teaching" means. But she shifts rather quickly to thoughts about how she might accommodate these pressures rather than resist them—and how accommodation might be good for her practice and for her students. It is a shift that captures in an instant the larger culture of Bayside Middle School.

> *JM:* Tell me about systems in the school that may be ratcheting up the pressure you're experiencing of needing to teach in data-focused ways.
> *AS:* You have all these state reviews and the [community school district] superintendent—all these reviewers come in, and it's like, what do they want to see? How do they want to see all this data presented? And that's the question that I feel gets asked over and over again, but nobody has an answer. We had a state review come in a few weeks ago, and they said they didn't see x, y, and z. But I *had* it, and nobody asked for it. In the past, whatever the students produced, whether spoken or written, was sufficient, and you used it to plan next steps, but I feel that it's gone beyond that now. They want it recorded—every single thing that's happening, and I was never asked for that before.
> *JM:* Who are "they"?
> *AS:* The administration.
> *JM:* Is it possible that some data doesn't have to be recorded, and can still meaningfully inform your teaching?

Here AS pauses briefly, and JM begins to realize that his question has struck her as the kind she would never ask her 7th graders—namely one that might invite them to let themselves off the hook.

> *AS:* [Smiling] You know, it's just like the kids. You tell them that they have to record things because they're not going to remember every little thing. *Yes*, if I had a conversation with so-and-so back in September and it was recorded by me in a more formal way, maybe it would be beneficial because then I could go back to it—whatever it was that I transcribed at that point. To be honest with you, I'm just beginning to think about that.
> *JM:* What helps you cope with the pressure [associated with data use in teaching]?
> *AS:* [Pause] I feel that we're all in the same conversation. I think it's teachers and administration that are included in this conversation. I think we're all realizing that this has to happen, and I think we're all on the same page of what do we do now. Where are we going with this? How do we make this happen?

Here it is: the crucial sense of "we-ness." This is the chief sign of *action space,* the term we use to depict a school successfully managing an insistent and complex innovation like data use in teaching. The management strategies may vary in specifics, but generally an action space accentuates goal-centered optimism and collaboration. It also undertakes local reframing of the innovation's larger theory of action (see Chapter 3), putting it into a contextually relevant form, as in "what do *we* mean by data use in teaching in *this* school?" with emphasis on the fact that there *is* a *we* here. This common goal ownership—together with a principal's inclination toward distributing leadership—can facilitate the creation of effective teams for action, and the raising of resources too (money, materials, professional knowledge, and civic buy-in). In the best of circumstances, the common goal ownership leads also to the solicitation of multiple forms of feedback to keep the action goals thoughtful and the action steps nimble (McDonald, 2014).

In this book, we distinguish between *action space* and *vortex*, which is the word and image we use to depict what happens when a challenging innovation like data use in teaching is just dropped in a cocksure way into an ill-prepared school or district. In physics, a vortex is a whirling, sucking mass of liquid or gas. Of course, the idea behind the innovation we are tracking in this book is that in teaching—as in manufacturing, medicine, sports, and other areas of contemporary life—data should be collected and consulted as an aid to design and action. And this is a very sensible idea—though only so long as one keeps an eye on its limits. For example, it does not mean that standardized data from annual and interim testing and off-the-shelf diagnostic tools can reveal in some definitive way what students like Khalil and Isaiah really know and need to learn at any given moment, or how teachers like AS need to act toward them at any moment. It does not mean that data can overcome the inherent predicaments and ambiguities of teaching and learning—the very dynamics of the wild triangle. In fact, data can only inform the management of these. Unfortunately, however, some champions of data use think otherwise. They overrate the power of data itself, and discount the role of people's understanding of it, and the challenges in their adapting their practices to it. And because these champions see data use in teaching as a matter of simple installation of a magical plug-in, they may see the failure of teachers to improve as willful and culpable. In such circumstances, what might have been a beneficial innovation becomes an unmanageable input, and a humiliating one too. The whirling and the sucking are the feeling and sound of local knowledge and local expertise collapsing, often for want of a system to fortify this knowledge and expertise.

Initially, we thought we had found a vortex at Bayside Middle School, but the more we studied the school, the more we found action space instead. As we said above, one early sign of it was the shift that AS made in the interview excerpt above from *me* to *we*. In retrospect, it seems possible to us that Principal Ernest Norris (EN) recommended AS to be the focal teacher for our Bayside study because he wanted us to see the team player in her. Vortex-style school reform efforts tend to prioritize the identification of exemplary practitioners so they can be emulated, and of failing ones so they can be flushed out. In action space, however—dependent as it is on shared optimism and persistence—priority attention goes to recognizing and increasing instances of collegiality and openness to improvement. Over time, other signs of action space emerged from our interviews of EN and other members of the Bayside administrative team.

Organized for Action

"Tell us about the school," researcher JM asked Principal EN on our first visit to Bayside. And EN plunged in: "The school's been here for 90 years, a fixture in this neighborhood. But then it was split into what I call the haves and the have-nots. The haves get 3's and 4's [passing and above on the annual state tests in literacy and math]. That's downstairs." Indeed, like many schools today in New York, Bayside shares a building with another middle school—an arrangement that is the product of more than a half century of small-school development in New York City, and of "co-location" of schools. Both building tenants are district schools (not charter), and they operate independently. But one uses test scores to "screen" its admissions, while the other does not. According to EN, the community school district superintendent who split the school up decided that the first stage of making a "bad" school "good" in a possibly gentrifying neighborhood is to create a protected space for the gentrifying families. "That's not my philosophy," EN added. "My philosophy is fix the problem, don't split it."

But he arrived years after the split, and became principal of the upstairs, "unscreened" school. "We are a Title 1 school," he told us, "around 92% free and reduced lunch," with a very large ELL population "at 42 or 43% officially ELL" (that is, serving emergent English speakers who have not yet passed a state English proficiency test). "And of the other 57%," he added, "the vast majority are former ELLs" (still emerging English speakers who have nonetheless "tested out" of the "official" category). Both groups, he added, include "lots of SLIFE students" (students with limited or interrupted formal education). These are often students who have experienced war or comparable sources of trauma. His students come, he said, from Mexico and the Dominican Republic (major sources of New York immigration), but also Ecuador, Honduras, El Salvador, and Colombia. And while "the vast majority are Latino—upper 80% range," others are from China and more recently Yemen.

At the start of this first interview in our 2-year Bayside study, JM told EN that we wanted to study data use in teaching at Bayside because others who know the school had told us that it is using data effectively.

> *EN:* I don't know that we're doing it *effectively*. I don't know that anybody's doing it really effectively. We used to do [teacher-maintained] data folios for each student, but it was so cumbersome to try to keep up when a teacher can have anywhere from 90 to 165 students. We do break the data down in terms of an item skills analysis from the testing, but we don't

really use the results effectively. I mean to use it effectively, you'd have to be able to differentiate on an individual basis. And I think you'd have to have a much smaller class size to be able to do that.

JM: When you think about data use in the school, what kinds of data are you thinking?

EN: You have data from [state standardized] testing. We did the citywide assessments [interim testing program] for baseline, and the kids did horribly. It didn't tell us much. We'll look at their NYSESLAT [state-mandated testing of English language learners], we'll look at last year's state exams. That and attendance. But does [state standardized] testing truly identify anything other than they got the question wrong? Does it show that there's a problem with language acquisition? Is it a learning disability versus a lack of formal education? You just need a lot more in-depth knowledge and analysis [of the situation] to be able to get a true picture. But it's helpful—I mean it gives you direction. And then we rely on in-class testing.

"In-class testing" in this context, we learned later, means assessments that teams of teachers in the same subject area write together, administer to their own students within agreed-upon windows, and later interpret together. This team-based authorship and debriefing is another sign of action space.

And there's so many programs out there, online programs. I mean, we tried to limit the number we use. And all these programs give you reports, and they self-level the students, and give you a baseline.

EN went on in this interview to talk about multiple such programs in use at the school—indeed, so many we initially thought, "Christmas tree school." This is a term Anthony Bryk and his colleagues used in a 1993 paper about types of school reform in Chicago. Here's how they define it:

Christmas tree schools are showcases. Their entrepreneurial principals become well known for their ability to garner new resources for their schools. . . . Unfortunately, this pursuit of new initiatives distracts the school community from a systematic examination of core operations. Additionally, there is little time to scrutinize the quality of the new programs or their cumulative effects on student learning (Bryk, Easton, Kerbow, Rollow, & Sebring, 1993, p. 14).

At the start of our study, we were particularly wary of finding the "Christmas tree" effect among our schools. This is because we found the schools partly by tracking their reputations among network leaders, and nothing builds a reputation higher in school leadership (as in many other occupations) than entrepreneurship and grant winning. EN, for example, is certainly entrepreneurial, and he has certainly amassed extra resources for his school, enough to invest in multiple programs to assist in data use, enough to be noticed by network leaders as doing so, and thus enough to be recommended to us. In a larger sense, too, we were wary about the tendency of some school leaders to think that investments in external programs—what we call the "material world"—can by themselves solve problems of schooling. In any case, we coded all of the programs EN noted in this first interview as *material world,* including something called the *Leader in Me* program, which JM first discovered that same day on a tour of the school, the *EL Education* curriculum, which we encountered in several of the middle schools we studied and uses the historical novel *Lyddie,* which figures in the wild triangle described at the beginning of this chapter. More about these two programs below.

First, however, it is important to note that in studying Bayside, we learned something that may seem obvious to many readers: that material investments are crucial to school improvement. No school facing the learning demands that Bayside faces every day has the capacity on its own to devise a curriculum, professional development program, assessments, technology platform, and cultural framework necessary to address such demands. The schools have to depend on others' inventions—ones they can literally buy into. At the same time, however, they cannot expect merely to buy them, then plug them in; whole-school improvement programs cannot run on their own. Programs like *Leader in Me* and *EL Education* need an action space. And on our first day at Bayside Middle School, we were not sure that the school had one. So JM's next question to EN came straight from James Spillane (2012, 2014). He had counseled us, and the other researchers that the Spencer Foundation had convened some months before, to look for purposeful organizational routines in the schools we studied. Data use in teaching is a social phenomenon, Spillane told us, and requires a social infrastructure.

> *JM:* Could you explain how the school is structured to support data use in teaching?
> *EN:* Well, I have a new Data Specialist, and she provides reports to five lead teachers—senior teachers, kind of like teaching coaches. One for ESL, one for ELA, one for science, one for social studies, and one for math. They are more experienced, they've worked themselves up. Other teachers respond to them. They get the item analysis breakdowns from the Data Specialist and then share them with their teams. They also look at student work.

Note that the phrase "look at student work" in the context within which EN used it here is professional jargon for treating samples of student work as data—for example, in order to understand from her math solutions a particular student's pattern of needs and strengths, or to understand from writing samples collected randomly across a couple of days how the school as a whole may be challenging its writers—or not challenging them (Blythe, Allen, & Powell, 2015; McDonald et al., 2013). As we would learn, data use in teaching at this school is as much focused on intimate data as it is on big-test data. Indeed, EN went on in this interview to talk about the limits of big-test data, even as he continued to describe the social structure:

> I mean the item analysis from the testing is only good at the beginning of the year to set things up. Then you have to have ongoing assessment. Different departments will do things a little differently. They may take a piece of student work and break it down, and look at best practices. Teachers do a lot of planning and team meetings—80 minutes on Monday and then 75 on Tuesdays. They also have common planning built into their schedules by department. We build in a lot of common planning time, time to work together.

Still, EN is aware that the school is judged on the basis of its progress in improving its students' big-test scores. JM asked him to characterize this progress, and he answered in terms of big-test performance bands.

> *EN:* They move. They move within the confines of what level they're at. They move within 1, and then from 1 to 2. We've just got to get over that next hump [3 is considered passing].
> *JM:* Are you hopeful about that?

At this point, EN began to talk about "we-ness," as well as several other features of action space, like optimism, flexibility, savviness in the procurement and use of resources, and persistence.

> [We've got] a pretty dedicated staff that works pretty hard. Not all, but most are willing to adapt to new things. You've got to push them sometimes. That's a big piece of it. And it's a collaborative environment for the most part. Very, very good with budget. I have a budget person who's even better than I am. We always try to plan ahead—1 year to 5 years. We try to work things out that way. And we're very flexible. Allow people to make mistakes. We're willing to try just about anything, but if something doesn't work, we'll drop it. The bottom line is why *not* do it? Don't worry [I tell the staff], *I'll* be the first to be fired.

The Leader in You

Following the interview above, EN arranged for JM to tour the school. His tour guide was Brianna, a 7th grader. We learned later that she was a member of the school's Lighthouse Team. Bayside is a Lighthouse (or model school) of the international *Leader in Me* Program. Brianna proved an excellent guide. She took JM on a long tour, stopping frequently to point things out, and she answered all his questions forthrightly and thoughtfully—even one touchy question. When she told him about the upcoming 7th-grade trip to the rainforest, he asked whether she was planning to go. She smiled, and said, "No, I have some documentation problems." The hallways she led him through were jammed with art and other student work, data graphs charting the school's progress in meeting certain goals (for example, 100% knowledge of the 8s and 9s multiplication tables), and murals and banners on numerous themes—including the rainforest. In one hallway, there was a *Leader in Me* installation, featuring portraits of leaders, one of them Beyoncé, and one of them whoever walks by (thanks to a floor-length mirror). The banner above the mirror declared "the leader in *you.*"

Leader in Me is a comprehensive school improvement program—a "material world" innovation introduced at Bayside 2 years before our arrival (www.theleaderinme.org). It derives from Stephen Covey's (1989) bestselling book, *The 7 Habits of Highly Effective People,* but focuses on elementary and middle school culture. It aims to foster the Covey habits in age-appropriate language, and in the context of schooling: initiative, responsibility, planning, prioritization, empathy, teamwork, and self-care. It does this in part through weekly Leadership Classes (akin to but more focused than the ubiquitous advisory classes in other middle schools); leadership activities (like training for and conducting tours); and lots of lesson plans, books, posters, banners, and—important for our purposes— student self-data-tracking, and student-led and data-rich family conferences. The program also features professional development efforts that aim to help teachers model the seven habits in interacting with each other as well as with their students. In its promotional material, the program claims plausibly that its effectiveness derives from the common language it instills across a school; the leadership it helps distribute to and among teachers and students; and the sense of agency that students gain within environments (elementary and middle schools) where their time, space, and activity are otherwise highly controlled.

Another of the Bayside School's important investments reinforce the *Leader in Me* focus on student agency—namely, its adoption of the *EL Education* literacy and social studies curriculum (eleducation.org). The Leader *in Me* culture derives from Stephen Covey and Mormonism, while the *EL* culture derives from Kurt Hahn and Outward Bound, but the two have much in common (James, 2000):

- An emphasis on character education and social emotional learning
- Promotion of leadership, empathy, and teamwork
- Nurturing of self-care and fitness

- Encouragement of students to take charge of their own personal goals and self-track progress in meeting them
- Support for data-rich, student-led family conferences

The two programs have some useful differences that Bayside takes advantage of. *EL* functions in many schools as a comprehensive school improvement program, but it can also function as a strictly academic resource, as it does here. And while Bayside had to pay for *Leader in Me* (roughly $70 per student in the first year of implementation, and $25 per in each subsequent year), *EL's* literacy curriculum is free (minus the cost of the trade books students read) thanks to New York State's selection of the curriculum as a recommended one, and to its decision to invest some of the funding it received from the Obama administration's *Race to the Top* program to make this curriculum available for free on a website called EngageNY (www.engageny.org).

THE BAYSIDE ACTION SPACE

The theory of action for data use in teaching as reframed at Bayside Middle School became clearest to us when we interviewed one of its chief reframers. We explore this interview in the next section. Then we conclude the chapter with a report on our final interview of focal teacher AS.

Two Pictures of the System

In an interview of the Bayside assistant principal, Suzie Welch (SW), JM asked her to describe the school's systems of data use in teaching, and he offered an array of subsystems she might take into consideration: data sources, administrative operations, teaching and learning activities, and teacher supports. Our research team knew by then that these subsystems, as well as others, figured in the overall Bayside data use system, but we wanted to know more about how they interrelated. In asking the question, JM offered a whiteboard diagram that seemed to SW to make data sources too central and administration too directive. See Figure 5.1, JM's design, for an approximation of his diagram.

Reacting quickly to the diagram, SW told JM that data is just information flow. It can't tell you, "teach this to that student." It gains meaning, she added, when it serves as input to an ongoing conversation. "In a regular DOE" [Department of Education] school, she added, administrators think they can just feed data to teachers. "However, we've decided that this does *not* work, so we have moved administrative systems into here first [pointing]."

Figure 5.1. Authors' initial model of the Bayside data use systems

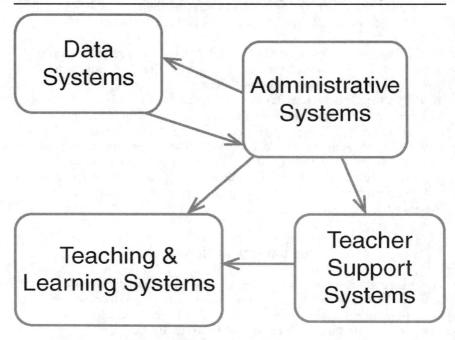

JM: So, when it comes to using data, you've merged administrative and teaching and learning systems?

SW: Yes, which then connect to the teacher support system. Because what we gather *together* through the [big-test] data, through looking at student work, through process, through rubrics, through baseline assessments—*these* create support systems and protocol which then go back into informational systems, and it becomes this type of cycle like this.

And at this point, SW drew on the whiteboard an emphatic circular connection among all the subsystems, suggesting that they are all interactive, not directional. See Figure 5.2, SW's correction, for an interpretation of her gesture.

SW: We found that if it is constant top down from administration through an information system, then these two systems [teaching and learning, and teacher support] were not responsive.

JM: Why do you think that's so?

SW: I've been in this role for 9 years, but I've been teaching in the New York City system for 15 years now. I've taught a gamut of subjects, and I've been all over the place as administrator. And within all of these quadrants, I'm constantly hearing *mandate*, and I think that's what a lot

Figure 5.2 SW's correction of the authors' initial model

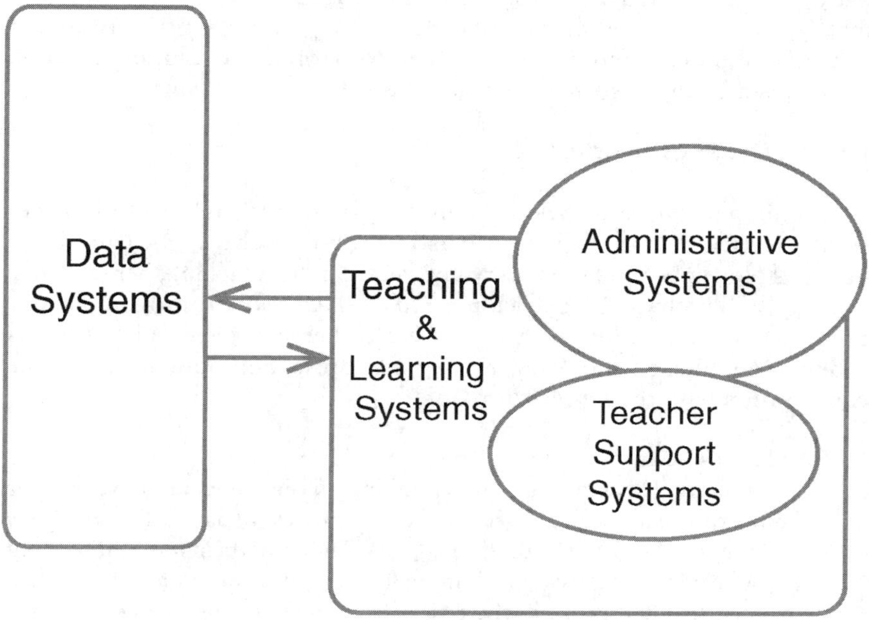

of teachers feel. It's not a collaborative system. Once it's a *mandate*, they lose autonomy, and then they won't do it. We've got the same kids that have always been here in the building and the neighborhood—within an environment where there's a strong union, within an environment that you can have uncooperative teachers, difficult teachers. When everyone asks us, "How are you doing this?" or, "How are you managing to do all these shifts [of practice toward data use]?" I say the biggest piece is the teacher support systems. Even that teacher that's very difficult to deal with—it's more of a personal feeling that creates the difficulty—their own process—and if that process is valued or noticed, then they do buy in.

JM: What do you mean?

SW: I would say it's been a lot of "Why do you feel this way? What can I help you with? What do you need me to do to figure out how to help you?" They have to see it for themselves. It can't be me telling them. Through that process, they also change within the classroom, because they notice that *I* [the teacher herself] am the one who creates the bad day.

There is nothing simple, nothing magical, about implementing an innovation like data use in teaching. It takes vision—though not just one person's; and it takes pushing, but the kind of pushing that respects pushing back, and accommodates constructive and collaborative adjustment. Ultimately, it takes an incorporation of multiple perspectives, a pragmatic use of available resources (plus a continual hunt for more), and a lot of reflection and adjustment. Is this what *we* mean to do? How about *this*?

Back to Our Focal Teacher

In the interview excerpt below, Annmarie Smith (AS) takes stock of her learning to use data in teaching. We had last observed her in the late spring; now it is November and she is very upbeat about her teaching, her students' learning, and both the *EL* curriculum and the *Leader in Me* program. In our previous interviews, she had never concealed her struggles, which lends us confidence that she is not exaggerating her satisfaction now. JM starts the conversation with the simplest prompt.

> *JM:* What's new?
> *AS:* It's funny. This morning, I was thinking I wish you would have seen me more this year. We finally streamlined the process of data collection. Now all the students have leadership binders. They had them last year too, but now they're being used much more, and this past week, we actually had student-led conferences where they led their own conference and were able to speak about their grades and their progress in class.

Here, as in interviews at some of our other schools, the success of data use in teaching is measured not just in big-test data gains, but in students' exercise of learning agency.

> I've really been more focused on having students create reading and writing goals. Now, for the second marking period, they're able to discuss their goals from the first marking period, how they felt they progressed, if they should keep them, slightly change them, change them altogether. They're tracking their progress now according to the learning targets. They're able to speak now to the rubric, and peer assessments: they're giving each other recommendations of how to move on. I feel like we finally came up with a system [of data use in teaching] that actually is feasible.

Checking to see if AS might confirm our emerging sense at this point of an action space at Bayside, JM asks her to account for the success she is describing.

> *AS:* A lot of hard work.
> *JM:* On everybody's part?

AS: Yeah.
JM: How about the *leadership* of it?

Here, JM uses the word as it is typically used in schools, but AS reframes it on the spot. She sees students as the leaders of this innovation.

You know what? The kids are taking ownership of their learning more than ever. They're really excelling, a lot of them. I think they like the fact that they're more responsible now than maybe in the past. They can see it. They can physically see it. They have something to show for it. Especially, I think, just putting the idea in their head: No, when you come up for conferences, *you're* gonna be the one telling your parent or guardian how you've progressed in this marking period. Your teacher is your advisor. She is taking the backseat to you.

As we suggested in Chapter 2, there can be no successful teaching without willful learning. So the idea that data use in teaching can be successful without data use in learning is shortsighted.

SUMMING UP

This dive goes deep into teaching and learning, where the complexities of practice are most evident, and where the pressure to innovate is also evident; for example, in the challenging nature of the text and methods the teacher uses. Then we move up to view the leadership at the top of the school and the vision it has cultivated and projects. Is this a vortex, where innovations fall apart? Or is it an action space where they grow stronger by means of distributed leadership and collective investment? An action space, we conclude, then we explore some of its features—a strongly articulated vision that comes from a distance but is reframed on site to suit the site; an artful pursuit of resources to invest in implementation; a critical capacity to exploit the material world without being exploited by it; a top leadership that knows how to delegate, and a middle leadership that knows how to empower; a teaching culture that proves open to learning; and finally, students persuaded to own their own progress.

Encouraging Student Agency

Data use in teaching that stops with the teacher, that fails to turn over data ownership to students, forfeits a good share of its potential impact on learning. After all, the inherent power of student performance data is that it can illuminate learning. Why wouldn't we want learners themselves to use such a tool? Yet the entire system of schooling seems in some sense devised to prevent this. It overemphasizes secrecy in testing, makes teacher discourse dominant in classroom speech, constrains most student initiative and even student movement, and puts the focus in data use on deficits and sanctions. Nevertheless, encouraged by their own sense of possibility and by some products from the material world, several of the schools we studied did take this direction—that is, they flipped some control of student performance data to students themselves. And they were surprised and pleased by the results. Even students with low test scores and reading levels, their teachers told us, seemed encouraged to work harder when they could see, understand, and track their performance data themselves.

To understand more about how to make this flip and why, read a 2014 book by Ron Berger, Leah Rugen, and Libby Woodfin, called *Leaders of Their Own Learning*. Berger is chief academic officer of EL (formerly Expeditionary Learning, and the same EL that featured in our Bayside deep dive). He is also a former 6th-grade teacher and master carpenter. Finally, he is a major curator of student work (See modelsofexcellence.eleducation. org/resources). In *Leaders*, Berger and his colleagues closely describe (and illustrate in a DVD) what they call student-engaged assessment. Here are its major steps:

- The school's teacher learning community maps in kid-friendly language a set of content-focused learning targets. Berger and his coauthors sensibly point out that students cannot own efforts to achieve learning goals that they have not seen and heard, or do not understand. In the mapping and discussing of learning targets, the teachers themselves come to understand them more deeply, and design their teaching to suit them more fully. The teacher learning community also promulgates character targets; for example, a willingness to assume responsibility for learning, a capacity for reflection, and a habit of revision.

89

- Next, teachers make time and space for data ownership. This involves a revolution in much ordinary classroom practice—replacing incessant teacher talk and worksheets with opportunities for students to study models, to work on projects of their own design, to self-assess, and to rehearse performances. Students also use the space and time to practice perspective taking, learning in the process how to offer and receive descriptive feedback. To see what the authors mean by descriptive feedback, see Berger's famous 6-minute Vimeo clip, "Austin's Butterfly" (vimeo. com/38247060) (also included in the DVD that accompanies *Leaders*).
- Teachers work within and across classrooms "to make learning public" by means of project exhibitions, authors' nights, public performances, the equivalents (across multiple disciplines) of science fairs, and other "celebrations of learning" (Berger et al., 2014, pp. 212–215).
- Finally, teachers teach students how to track and interpret their own performance data. And they empower them with preparation and coaching to lead their own data-focused family conferences. In the DVD accompanying the Berger et al. (2014) book, see Kansas kindergartener Trinity lead a conference on her learning progress with her mom, dad, and teacher all present and following her lead.

Like all major innovations in teaching and learning, this one is complex and takes time to grow. Moreover, as the above steps suggest, it is highly reliant on other New Directions we explore elsewhere in this book—especially distributed leadership (following Chapter 4), a teacher learning community (following Chapter 6), and opening up space and time for learning (following Chapter 7).

A Vortex at South Falls

In Chapter 5, we described the characteristics of action space. These include communal commitment, coordination of resources, teamwork, optimism, and trust. Action space is created and spurred along by strong and inclusive leadership—the kind that can reframe an innovation to fit an actual context, and ensure openness to feedback and appropriate revision (McDonald, 2014). It is a tough package to assemble, and no school we've studied has gotten it perfectly into place. In this sense, action space may be more image than condition. Still, with enough of the package in place and with the image in mind, a school can take a cocksure innovation like data use in teaching, and turn it into something systemically useful and ultimately beneficial for students. In describing action space in Chapter 5, we contrasted it with an organizational state that seems its opposite. Instead of a preface to change or renewal, what we call *vortex* can be a preface to collapse. We named this kind of school context after the term in physics that describes a whirling or sucking gas or liquid. This seems an appropriate metaphor for what can happen when a complex innovation like data use in teaching is pressed on a school ill-equipped to manage it: adults struggle as if in a windstorm, and children lose opportunity as if down a drain.

Vortex is the focus of this chapter. In this deep dive, we see intentions, language, teaching, and learning spin out of control. We draw the contrast with the previous chapter not to make a good school/bad school comparison, but to portray the complexity of schooling from two different perspectives: with the right attitudes and resources in place, and in their absence. Ultimately, both chapters portray an innovation that must be carefully implemented, and cannot simply be plugged in. People allergic to complexity shouldn't get involved in school reform.

SOUTH FALLS ELEMENTARY SCHOOL

Like many other schools in New York City, South Falls faces multiple challenges that seem to beg for action space. Virtually all of its students experience poverty-impacted lives in one of the city's poorest neighborhoods. Almost all are still emerging speakers of English, with a third still formally classified as English Language Learners. And a fifth of the school's students are classified as students with special needs. The principal who welcomed our research, Deanna Reid [DR], was the middle of three principals in 3 years. Rapid leadership turnover, or churn, generally precludes action space because leadership drives action space, and is typically the guarantor of the resources that feed it (Bryk et al., 2010). And churn can also demoralize staff and students. They may think, what's the point of action? The New York City DOE "snapshot" of South Falls for the 2014–2015 school year, when DR was principal, confirms our finding that action space was missing then. Educational leadership was rated poor, and teacher collaboration as well as family–community ties and overall trust were rated only fair. Predictably—given the school's proportions of emerging bilinguals and students with special needs—the school underperformed with respect to citywide proficiency averages that year in both literacy (though only by 9%) and math (only by 5%). However, the school's record in moving underskilled students *toward* proficiency (an important indicator for schools serving high proportions of students still learning academic English) was worse. Moreover, in literacy, students who had previously scored as proficient were much less likely to maintain proficiency than students in other city schools.

Reframing the Innovation

In all the schools we studied, principals in collaboration with other school leaders reframed the innovation we call data use in teaching in attempts to fit it to their schools' contexts. That is, they interpreted something handed down from higher-up policy levels with the school's history and mission in mind, as well as its specific challenges and opportunities. And they used this new frame to organize implementation efforts: to inform and enlist teachers, parents, and students; to identify and procure supportive resources; and to set local goals. In some schools we studied, this reframing proved energizing. But here, it proved enervating, and leadership turnovers exacerbated the impact.

South Fall's principal, DR, a fresh leader in what would turn out to be a churn situation, might have led her seriously challenged faculty (seriously challenged with respect to content knowledge and pedagogical knowledge) with a sense of optimism, a cultivation of outside resources, and a call for collaboration and knowledge sharing. Instead, she took a more fearful than hopeful path, emphasizing the state and city's threat of closing the school and "excessing" its teachers. In New York City, "excessed" teachers from a school that has been closed can be hired by other schools, though they may carry a stigma in the job marketplace for having worked in a failing one. Therefore, they may end up in a pool of teachers who work in other schools as substitute teachers. In taking the fearful path, DR was following a citywide, statewide, and national preoccupation with installing data use in teaching with the threat that it had *better* work, as if the availability of content knowledge and pedagogical knowledge were irrelevant, easily purchased, or achievable by will power alone. DR was also herself a victim of fear. She told one member of our research team, Nora Isacoff (NI), that standardized test data is being used to give extra money to favored schools, and to close down other schools. Data is "being used to judge teachers," she said, and teachers teaching large numbers of English language learners are particularly vulnerable, she added.

> When they came up with No Child Left Behind, the policy makers were only thinking of one type of population, and they were not thinking about the ELLs. If they would have thought about the ELLs, they wouldn't have done that. But then there's also a political agenda that's been around for years. If you have an ELL kid that comes in, after a year and a day, you have to test them on the state English exam. But it's impossible that in one year and one day, an individual is going to know the language at the same level as their peers that have been here all their lives, born and raised. So that's unfair.

DR went on to acknowledge in this interview that the DOE had recently begun taking more account than before of within-performance-band growth—for example, favorably viewing a student moving from a low 1 or 2 to a higher 1 or 2. But she added that growth was still not given enough weight, and then jumped to a complaint about South Falls teachers' lack of technological savvy.

> One of the things with data, right, is that you need to be tech-savvy, you know? And I wouldn't say that my staff is there. Right? And that's part of the training that we're doing, we're currently doing, is teaching them. We were teaching them how to do a PowerPoint. That's the level they're at. Excel: that's another class that we have to teach them. So, we have to teach them how to do Excel and how to manipulate that. We did a class on Google—what is Google, Google Docs, having a Gmail account, what is uploading and downloading docs, how to create a doc.

Her point makes sense here, but it involves a condition that can be ameliorated, and she acknowledges as much by saying that she has organized learning opportunities that address it. But her tone emphasizes deficit over opportunity.

Then DR begins to reveal her implicit theory of data use in teaching. As in some other theories we discovered in other schools, her theory overestimates the power of big-test data, and of ARIS—the data warehouse we described in Chapter 3 that New York City was then using. She tells NI that it offers a far more precise map of learners' needs than, in fact, it ever did. If there is a single worst misperception that plagues data use in teaching, this is it: the illusion of precision. But DR claims that the problem is not illusory precision, but rather teachers' inability to understand and act on precise directions.

> *DR:* The teachers receive a copy of the spreadsheet that comes from the DOE, from ARIS. It's a skill analysis per kid, you know, for every little skill for math, for every little skill for ELA, what did the kid do, how did your kids do?
>
> *NI:* What would you say is your overall theory of how data can be used in teaching?
>
> *DR:* [Data] plays a role as to the materials that you choose to teach the children, and the everyday decisions that the teachers choose to make to improve children and help them move along. So, data is a real big part of it.
>
> *NI:* How would you compare your idea of data use in teaching with teachers' ideas of it?
>
> *DR:* I look at it from a different perspective. I think of it as a whole. And I look for patterns as a whole: school-wide, across the grades, across the content areas, whereas a teacher usually would look at it from a teacher's perspective, you look at more of an individual. What are the needs of the class and then the needs of the individuals?
>
> *NI:* How do the teachers determine these needs?
>
> *DR:* They do an assessment, and whatever the kids are not exactly mastering, they go revisit that stuff.

Some of the other schools we studied used this strategy too. We call it regrouping and reteaching. But observing it across several contexts, we found it worse than insufficient. This is because it tends to reduce the content of learning to test items (instead of the broader knowledge or skills that the items were meant to measure), and also because it tends to reduce pedagogy to worksheets that mimic standardized tests.

Planning by Design

One day at South Falls, NI observed a 4th-grade team meeting among four teachers and an outside literacy consultant. The purpose of the meeting was to plan a lesson together that the teachers would later teach in their respective classes. At the beginning of the meeting, the consultant explained to the teachers that she was there as a coach for their planning, to make sure they are "doing it by design and not haphazardly." The mood in the room, as usual at this school, was tense, and it seemed to NI that the teachers were trying to figure out what exactly the consultant meant by this remark, and how they might participate in this planning effort in a way that avoided appearing "haphazard."

One teacher began the co-planning process by suggesting that their class-es read *The Tarantula Scientist,* a nonfiction text about a spider expert (Montgomery & Bishop, 2004). Another teacher tried to figure out if this would be an appropriate choice: "What is the Lexile of *Tarantula Scientist*?" she asked. The first teacher said, "890." "Okay," the other replied, "that puts it right at 4th/5th grade. Not the F&P level [Fountas & Pinnell, 2016]," she added. She went on to explain that a Lexile level takes into account only the length of words and number of compound sentences. "It doesn't have anything to do with comprehension. It's all the decoding world." Her remark seemed aimed at demonstrating to her colleagues and the consultant that *she,* at least, knew the standards they were supposed to meet. And, in combination with the consultant's warning about "haphazard" planning, the remark undercut from the beginning the possibility of genuinely joint planning. It seemed to turn the meeting into a kind of contest.

Another teacher asked whether the assignment based on the text they might choose should be "comparative" or "persuasive based on information text," and the other teachers started naming standards they thought the assignment should adhere to: "It should be content-rich." "It should be the anchor standard." And the consultant pointed out that "deconstructing the standards becomes fodder for assessment and mini-lessons." The phrases multiplied, but they all seemed empty, gratuitous. Meanwhile, all of the teachers had begun by then to look lost. Some sighed loudly. And the consultant, a young and polished graduate student, shot NI a few eye rolls—as if she too felt the need to participate in the contest. "I know," she seemed to say with her eyes, "that these teachers do not know what they need to know."

Soon, something like bickering broke out, though again it seemed to involve points that no one in the room really cared much about. The consultant said that students need to learn both content knowledge and skills. One teacher said that knowing what makes a good supporting detail in an essay is an example of content knowledge, but the consultant replied that no, this is an example of a skill. The teacher conceded that, okay, this is a 4th-grade skill, but another teacher said no, it's a 5th-grade skill. And so on. Some of the bickering concerned the wording of New York State Learning Standards, and of rubrics associated with them—for example:

Teacher A: In 3rd grade they write a statement, but in 4th and 5th grade, they have to restate their opinion.
Teacher B: But in the 3rd-grade rubric, they have to restate.
Teacher A: But do they have to restate their reasons or just their opinion?
Teacher B: I'll look it up.

Meanwhile, no one mentioned student performance data. No one even raised the question of what their students *evidently* need to learn or be able to do. There was no student work on the table or on the whiteboard. There was no spreadsheet to refer to. The planning began with *The Tarantula Scientist*, and then descended rapidly into a conversation that seemed remote from the children. It is, of course, important for 4th-grade teachers to talk about rich materials they have found, and to discuss the nuances of the particular standards that are intended to guide their teaching, but it is far better to hold such discussions with the students' learning strengths and needs virtually present in the form of work samples and other performance data. Otherwise, *planning* loses its crucial third angle. It needs to connect teacher, subject, and learners.

Suddenly, at one point in the conversation, the consultant made a pronouncement that seemed to startle the other members of the group:

> *Consultant:* For the culminating project, they will do some research and create a persuasive piece.
>
> *Teacher A:* (repeating verbatim) For the culminating project, they will do some research and create a persuasive piece.
>
> *Teacher B:* Let me see if I understand, because I understand better with examples. So, they might choose a panda, do research on it, and then that will be the basis for their persuasive piece?
>
> *Teacher A:* I have a student who is so bright, but he can't read. So, I would hate to see him do poorly on a writing assignment just because he can't read.
>
> *Consultant:* But for me, assessing writing isn't only about a high-stakes test. It's also thinking about how does their reading and their content knowledge translate into their writing.
>
> *Teacher A:* Sometimes you have a student with a low reading level, and then that affects their writing.

It is likely that Teacher A has made a very important point here, though too haltingly. If she had dared to be more explicit, then everyone might have grappled with an absurd mismatch: the one between the phrase "create a persuasive piece" and the fact that one 4th grader cannot read—presumably cannot decode, never mind *en*code persuasively. Teacher A comes close to saying what she's really thinking: "Are you *kidding*? Can we talk about the fact that I have a 4th grader who can't read!?" However, she cannot quite step over some invisible line that prevents her from saying this. The tenor of this "planning meeting" does not encourage this step. Her colleagues do not invite it. And the consultant seems oblivious to the need for it.

TEACHING IN A VORTEX

The teacher at South Falls whom we observed most often was Ivan Gonzalez [IG]. Experienced and confident, he is well regarded by his peers, and serves as a member of the School Leadership Team, a committee of staff members and parents who meet regularly to plan and monitor overall school improvement. In interviews with us, and in our observations of meetings in which he participated, IG appeared competent. But his teaching seemed to us all whirlwind. Walking into his classroom, one felt a sudden loss of space and air. Walls were blanketed with student work and performance data charts, but in a fashion that turned information into meaningless shapes and colors. And the room buzzed constantly with teacher talk turning even independent or otherwise "silent" reading into what can only be called noise. Other sounds (of student chatter, moving desks, and so on) were also elevated in this room, creating cacophony. Absorbing it, students became fidgety. Some threw pencils in the air or spun highlighters on their desks.

Substituting Talk for Teaching

During one visit, NI, arriving during the short interval between math and English language arts, found IG expressing frustration with his students for not finishing their math tests on time. He seemed desperate. "You need to use your time efficiently if you want to do well on the state test!" he exclaimed, literally wringing his hands and pacing. However, he soon calmed down, and pivoted to what he later described to NI as "guided reading," but to his students as "independent reading." In fact, the better term might have been *common silent reading with many interruptions intended to offer guidance*. By any name, it proved to be a poor instructional move.

The text IG used was *The Birchbark House* by Louise Erdrich (1999). Set in 1847, the story centers on 7-year-old Omakayas, a member of the Anishinabe (later, Ojibwa) tribe, as she encounters white settlement and cares for her family during a smallpox epidemic. IG told NI that the novel was originally intended for 7th-graders, but that ReadyGEN—a Pearson curriculum used by South Falls—included it in its 4th-grade curriculum. In fact, the novel is promoted as an exemplar for 4th and 5th grade in the Common Core State Standards (2017), though some students do read it in middle school. To accommodate the needs of his English language learners, IG told NI, he asks them to read 5 pages a day instead of 50 as ReadyGEN suggests. For this 256-page book, IG's pace would require 2 months or more.

IG began his peculiar mix of "silent" and "guided" reading by reviewing the previous chapter with students, reminding them that "the fancy word in the book for plan is *scheme*," and asking them to make predictions about what will happen in the upcoming chapter.

IG: What do you think will happen next?
Student 1: I think things will go badly.
Student 2: I agree that things will go badly.
Student 3: I don't think that things will go badly.

IG: Oh, so we have a disagreement here. You think the girls are going to
   fight. You're basing that on what you already know about the characters.

Here, we see IG miss an opportunity to encourage students to elaborate
on their predictions, to support them with evidence from the text, and to
engage in discussion with each other. Instead of asking them to explain what
they meant, he inferred it himself. This type of missed opportunity was ram-
pant across most of our study sites at both 4th- and 7th-grade levels. We associate the problem with a fear among some teachers of entering unfamiliar
content territory. IG also tended in the lessons we observed to ask questions
he had already planted answers for, as in eliciting the word "evidence" by
asking students, "What do you need to look for when reading? It begins with
an E." He did this in the name of what he called "inquiry-based learning."
But, in fact, asking many questions with predetermined answers—though it
serves to keep a lesson tightly on track—can hamper genuine inquiry. It is a
kind of oral worksheet.

   See what scheme the characters come up with. Does the scheme work?
   What evidence do you have to see whether it worked? Evidence has to
   be the basis. Of course you have your own opinion, but evidence has to
   be the basis.

IG also asked students to underline a minimum of three "key details"
while reading—presumably in relation to their sense of an emerging scheme
and whether or not it worked—and he told them that once they had finished
reading, they would work in small groups to write up an answer to the
question. This task seemed straightforward enough, and students appeared
to understand what was expected, and how the process would proceed.
But then the wind blew in. Here is an account from the transcript of NI's
observation notes:

   Students began reading, and there was quiet for about 15 seconds.
   Then IG began. "You should be around the top of page 56," he called
   out. "That area. I'm just giving you guys a pace." And then he started
   moving around the room, whispering additional prompts to individual
   students. A minute later, he called out again: "Some of your predictions
   are happening on page 56." And then 30 seconds after that: "To give
   you a heads up, toward the bottom of page 57, her plan starts to take
   form." He paced, and called out again: "Remember, you can use your
   pencil to make the markings. Just to give you guys the pacing, you
   should be at the bottom of 57 heading to 58 if you're focused, on task."
   And he repeated this again for any students who might be immersed in
   the book and might not have absorbed his advice: "You should be at the
   bottom of 57, heading to 58, if you're focused, on task."

Then 10 seconds later: "You should be in that zone. 58, 59. That's the safe zone. On 58, there's definitely key details about her plan. Definitely key details there." He stopped talking for another 10 seconds, glanced at his copy of the book, and modeled interest for any students who were listening: "Wow. Hmm. Oh wow! Interesting! Careful with 58. The plan is on 58. Just giving you guys a heads up. They take action on 58."

After another 15 seconds of silence, he carried on more: "59, you're going to read about the effect of that scheme. Some things that happen as a result of that scheme. 58, 59. 58, the plan is hashed out. 59, some of the effects of that plan. Great, most of you are on task. You're building stamina. Staying on task for a longer amount of time. Reading independently for a longer amount of time. 58 is the plan. 59 is some of the effects of that plan. 60 is the end of that episode. It wasn't that long! Again, on 58 the plan is hashed out. On 59, some of the effects of that plan. And on 60 is the conclusion, the result. How does it all end up? Those are the three parts. 58, you should have found the details of that plan. 59, they're enacting the plan, carrying out the plan, and on 60, how does it all turn out? Those are the three pieces to the episode."

He repeated his "guidance" a few more times, then encouraged everyone to finish up: "Some of us read at different paces. I see some heads up. It's okay. While you're waiting for your groups, go back and read what you underlined. Read what stood out. And see if the details that you underlined match the task. Are they going to provide you with the evidence to discuss the task?"

During the 15 minutes in which students read five pages, there was perhaps a total of 1 minute when IG was not speaking.

IG employed a similar hands-*very*-on approach throughout our observations of his lessons, exemplifying the opposite of the teaching behavior we identified in Chapter 2 as *walking away;* that is, setting students to work in a clear and supportive way, then physically and verbally distancing oneself to give them independent work space. In another lesson, for example, he told students to choose any chapter in the book the class was reading:

You're going to choose any chapter of the book. I'm not going to assign you the chapter. You have to pick any chapter you want. You're going to choose one piece of evidence of character traits. Evidence can be what they said, what they did, or what they felt.

This is a good prompt—one that might cue the teacher next to walk away, as students got to work. But here, just as soon as students picked up their books to choose a chapter, IG completely changed the assignment:

We're tight on time, so work with your partners. Pick a *page* that has evidence. Can I give you a hint? Chapter 5 has a lot of evidence. Now you have to pick one piece of evidence. It could be something they say, something they do, or something they feel.

It seemed often in IG's lessons as if time were so tight that schedule mattered more than task. In this instance, there was just enough time for IG to give students the *right* answer and reiterate it for any students who might need a second hearing, and this substituted for the original task that involved students reading, exploring, and figuring something out. *That* task vanished down some invisible drain.

How to explain IG? It is certainly possible that he lacks the kind of content knowledge (for example, of history or of reading), and/or pedagogical content knowledge (for example, of how to lead the exploration of a text), to perform competently the job he has. It is also possible that he lacks important personal capacities in a teacher: a capacity to listen, to wait, to keep still. However, he certainly does not lack a belief in the innovation we are studying—at least so far as we know, given what he told us. But we are also alert to the possibility that in this school—as in all the others we studied— some of our research participants, knowing we were studying an innovation pushed by city, state, and the federal government, might have seemed more favorable to it than they actually were. Moreover, we also think that certain characteristics of this school at the time we studied it exacerbated gaps in the sensible pursuit of this innovation: the race toward implementation, the emphasis on failure, and the absence of a genuine professional learning community.

From the Teacher's Perspective

In a series of interviews of IG, NI pressed him to articulate his theory of action with respect to data and teaching. Here is what he had to say, much of it magical:

> NI: Do you think data also informs work that you do with your colleagues— for example, in grade-level planning meetings?
> IG: The school and the principal look at how the 4th grade performed, and they always do that printout, the little bars, so, yes, it does affect us. Oh yeah. And then they'll say, you know, 4-A did well in this area compared to 4-B, so yes, it does affect.
> NI: Does it affect your instruction?
> IG: My instruction is based upon the data. That lets me know, hmm, I need to pick up the speed, I need to slow it down, which areas do I need to focus on. I love it, especially now with the testing, the item analysis. It pinpoints for us exactly which standard they're lacking proficiency in.

> That guides my instruction. So I know cause and effect. Oh, they had a 90 percentile? I'll still touch it, but now, mmm, word meaning, they only got 23%, so I know which areas then to focus on.

NI asked IG specifically which data he was referring to, and he said "the common core test"—that is, the New York State test that his students had taken in the spring of their 3rd grade. At this point, however, his students were well into their 4th grade. Can a teacher construct effective lessons now from 6-month-old data? One can imagine that IG might have gotten a better sense of whether to "pick up the speed" or "slow it down" by observing and interacting with his 4th-grade students, rather than by consulting old records. NI tried to push him on this point by asking what he typically learns from standardized tests that he cannot glean from his own classroom assessments.

> The rubric for classwork is more general. The standardized tests really pinpoint the Common Core—exactly what standards they need to know by this age, by this grade. Classroom assessment, it's the bigger picture. Oh, he's a good writer, he's wow! But the standardized test gives us the standards.

We see here again an inflated sense of the validity of standardized testing. In one interview, NI asked IG about his approach to reading instruction, and he replied that his approach is based on how "low" his students are, as measured by standardized state test data, and also standardized classroom-based data.

> I have their running records from last year, and based on the running records, a lot of these kids are at an M [level of text complexity, per Fountas & Pinnell, 2016]. By 4th grade, they should be at a Q at least. But these kids are low. They're at M, N, O, or P. And their state test scores are also low. A lot of them are a 1 [on a performance range from 1 (lowest) to 4]. I only have six 3's out of 26 [students]. And I have no 4's. So that's why I have to do guided reading with them. You don't usually do guided reading with 4th grade, but I have to. [Actually, we saw guided reading in 7th-grade classrooms, though IG likely means the kind of guided silent reading we recounted above.]

NI asked IG to elaborate on how students' standardized data levels impact his approach to reading instruction, and he explained, "I have to sit with them, help them figure out what page things are on. Help them with fluency. Because, based on the item analysis [of state exam performance], it's fluency and comprehension that they're low on. And we know that if they don't have fluency, they can't comprehend, so I have to help them with that."

Like many of the teachers we observed, IG is intent on using data to drive his instruction, but he doesn't feel clear about how to do so effectively, and he relies ultimately on grouping. Referring to a lesson at the beginning of our second year of the study, IG described his overall plan for data-driven instruction:

> *IG:* For now, it's all heterogeneous. But then in October, I will start dividing them up by levels so that some do guided reading and some don't.
>
> *NI:* Okay, and when you do that, how will you figure out who goes in what group?
>
> *IG:* Running Records.
>
> *NI:* Is this the Running Records from last year or you're doing new ones?
>
> *IG:* We do them in October, then February, and then May. But you'll notice, I had all my lowest students in the front on the carpet. The rest was heterogeneous. But that way, I can keep an eye on them. You could see, they were the ones who were jumping around. But I don't tell them they're the low ones, because they say if you tell them, that affects their self-esteem. But they'll figure it out once I start pulling them out. But you see, I don't tell them it's for the exam.

One pattern that recurred in our observations of IG's practice was an expressed discomfort—even apology—for what he called "fancier words." For example, he would tell his students, "I know these are fancier words!" or "We have to use these fancier words!" The irony in his use of this phrase and the tone he gave it, is that his students—nearly all still struggling to gain what linguists call an academic vocabulary in English—really needed to learn "fancier" words. This is because vocabulary size is one of the greatest predictors of academic success (Zwiers, 2014). So, he clearly needed to learn how to feel comfortable introducing them to "fancier" words, and to abandon any embarrassment he may have felt himself in using them. A good coach might have taught him this; first, by pointing out the problem and the rationale for facing up to it, and then by leading him through rehearsals of how to use "fancier" words in inviting ways. The coach might have been one of his colleagues, for example, or perhaps a consultant more skillful and respectful than the one we observed at the planning meeting portrayed above.

In the end, it seemed to us that IG's data use practices were overwhelmed by fear that it may not just be his students who are failing, but he himself—despite his experience and his good intentions. His practice on the surface seems directed by policies he embraces frantically, but policies cannot successfully direct practice. They can only inform them. Practitioners need to direct their practices themselves, informed by both policies and their active engagement in exploring what their students need. They do this best in environments in which hope trumps fear, in which colleagues help each other and learn continually from each other, and in which they can gain access as needed to skillful and thoughtful outside help. At the time we studied their work, IG and his colleagues lacked such an environment. Hence the vortex we describe above.

Yet there is always the possibility of action space emerging even from what seem poor prospects. It depends on the availability of the right leadership and the possibility of the right resources. While we collected no data ourselves from South Falls Elementary School during the 2015–2016 school year, some New York City Department of Education (NYCDOE) indicators rose then—especially ones we and others regard as leading indicators of improvement in student learning (Bryk et al., 2010). The rating on school leadership, given a change in leadership, jumped from poor to good, and the ratings on family–community ties and on trust both moved from fair to good. Perhaps the third principal in 3 years proved to be the right leader. Time will tell whether she can assemble the right resources, and build the kind of teacher learning community the school needs.

SUMMING UP

In this third of four deep dives into data use in teaching in New York City, we illuminate a condition we call *vortex*—when champions of a complex innovation push too hard and fast on a school that lacks the leadership and pedagogical skills to make good sense of it. The principal here, new to the job and nervous in the assignment, projects doubt rather than hope in the possibility of implementation. An outside consultant acts in ways that demean the school's teachers and end up fostering defensiveness rather than a teacher learning community. And a focal teacher expressing eagerness about the innovation stumbles badly in his teaching for want of pedagogical knowledge (for example, of how to ask questions), and pedagogical content knowledge (for example, of how to scaffold his students' reading in content areas). The chapter ends, however, with some signs of improvement—in leadership, and in an equally important lubricant for innovation, trust.

Building a Teacher Learning Community

Across our sample of nine schools, progress in implementing data use in teaching proved invariably linked to progress in building a schoolwide teacher learning community. This makes sense because data use in teaching requires a lot of teacher learning, and schools are not ordinarily well organized for teacher learning. Major studies have demonstrated that in the U.S., schools tend to isolate teachers (Goodlad, 1984; Jackson, 1968; Lortie, 1975; Sizer, 1984), severely limiting one of the best sources for professional learning, namely collegial contact. Recent generations of school reformers have worked to instill more collegiality in U. S. schooling, and researchers who have studied their efforts have found real gains (Fullan, 2016; Little, 1982; McLaughlin & Talbert, 2006; Newmann & Wehlage, 1995). Still, in a 2011 national survey of 10,212 U.S. P–12 teachers, the teachers reported spending on average only 15 minutes of their teaching day interacting with colleagues (Scholastic & Bill and Melinda Gates Foundation, 2012).

Districts and networks of schools have historically tried to compensate for this loss of collegial contact through organized professional development (PD). The largest portion of PD involves what are called workshops, though they are rarely hands-on, and sometimes just PowerPoint presentations. These may happen on one or two whole days a year, or in briefer after-school meetings. They are typically led by an outside consultant or an administrator, and are often limited with respect to follow-up. A 2014 survey by the Boston Consulting Group and the Gates Foundation found that 49% of the 132 teachers they surveyed were dissatisfied with such workshops (in contrast to 22% who were satisfied, and the rest who were "neutral") (McBride, Bailey, & Lautzenheiser, 2015). This finding is hardly surprising. Workshop-based PD has long been disparaged by teachers, who say they prefer "personalized . . . teacher-driven . . . hands-on . . . sustained" PD—particularly presented by someone who is still a teacher, and who treats the other teachers in the room as fellow professionals (Scholastic & Bill and Melinda Gates Foundation, 2012, p.4).

In response to this critique, many districts have introduced "collaborative PD," involving professional learning communities often called "PLCs" (DuFour, 2016; DuFour, Eaker, & DuFour, 2005). Indeed, PLCs (standing groups that meet regularly to engage in professional learning activity) are now the dominant form of PD in terms of hours devoted to them. The problem, however, is that teachers like PLCs even less than they like workshops (a whopping 56% dissatisfied, and only 11% satisfied, with the "neutrals" in between). The reasons for dissatisfaction, the surveyed teachers report, is that PLCs often devolve into administrative briefings; are often not well planned or facilitated; and are often disconnected from teaching (McBride et al., 2015). In other words, collaborative PD often turns out to be neither collaborative nor useful.

However, it doesn't have to be this way. What is needed instead?

We call for the following four practices of school-based professional learning. All are hard to put in place, but worth the effort. To our list, we add recommended resources.

1. In many places, teachers have to take charge of their own learning at the school level—including which outside consultants they need if any, and how to use them. They have to make a deal with administrators to butt out of their teacher learning community, and let teachers run it. These are the places that lack—for now—a collaborative culture. In return for the right to self-regulate their learning, the empowered teachers have to commit to taking responsibility for student learning too, and to make no excuses for themselves when their efforts fall short. See *Leading for Powerful Learning*, the 2012 book by Angela Breidenstein, Kevin Fahey, Carl Glickman, and Frances Hensley, for ideas about how to design and manage a teacher learning community that takes collective responsibility for its students' success in learning.

2. Taking responsibility for student learning requires something that teachers do not always think about: inducing student cooperation. Indeed, some teachers resist going this far, and thus rule out students who need them the most, who have become resistant to teaching for reasons that range from simply previous experience of learning failure to racism, abuse, or other trauma. As we pointed out in Chapter 2, however, inducing cooperation even among highly resistant students is inherent in the job of teaching. For inspiration about how to embrace this dimension of the work, read David Kirkland's (2013) book, *A Search Past Silence: The Literacy of Young Black Men*; Kathy Greeley's (2000) book, *Why Fly that Way?*; and Bill Ayers and illustrator Ryan Alexander-Tanner's (2010) book, *To Teach: The Journey, in Comics*.

3. A key function of a teacher learning community is to update and curate content knowledge. This starts with dispelling the idea that only "weak" teachers need to update their content knowledge. Indeed, all teachers need to do this on a continual basis, because

content across all fields continually changes. And a key way they can do this is to embrace their roles as curators and sharers of content across their community. Here, the Internet affords a huge opportunity, including access to other curators' collections—for example, *The Teaching Channel* (www.teachingchannel.org), with hundreds of high-quality videos of high-quality, content-rich teaching; *Edmodo*, a popular potpourri of images, videos, and other content-immersive opportunities (www.edmodo.com); and the American Federation of Teachers' collection of lesson plans at *Share My Lesson* (sharemylesson.com).

4. Teachers have to work within the context of their learning community to ensure equity in teaching and learning. This means learning how to engage productively in what Glenn Singleton calls courageous conversations about the ways that race—as well as class, gender, disability, sexual orientation, and other human distinctions—figure in and sometimes interfere with a teaching and learning community. Key resources include Singleton's (2015) book, called *Courageous Conversations*, and Christopher Emdin's (2016) book, *For White Folks Who Teach in the Hood, and the Rest of Y'all Too.*

CHAPTER 7

Implementation at the Waterfront

Throughout this book, we have suggested that the innovation we call data use in teaching must be reframed to suit the school context that it enters, and then adapted—in a mix of fidelity and invention unique to each school—to actual capacities, needs, and conditions. Indeed, while the impact of the innovation on learning outcomes varied considerably across the schools we studied, all engaged to some degree in reframing. None tried just to plug in data use in teaching and let it run. However, none of the other schools went quite so far as the Waterfront Middle School did toward full *implementation*. We use this term as Milbrey McLaughlin (1987) does in a classic paper on the subject of how policy and practice actually intersect. Implementation, she argues, is what happens when users of an innovation down to the street level (in this case, the classroom level) adopt and adapt an innovation in ways that significantly alter previously existing systems. In this deep dive, we explore this phenomenon.

WATERFRONT MIDDLE SCHOOL

Unlike many other poverty-impacted and racially isolated schools in New York City, the Waterfront School is not red-lined by a zip code full of such schools. It is located within a gentrifying neighborhood. Yet it is bound by its history of serving children and families who live in low-income public housing, substandard private housing, or homeless shelters. New families in this neighborhood—who live in repurposed industrial buildings, or gleaming new high-rises—are typically zoned into other schools.

The Waterfront School was founded in 2004, part of a decades-long and city-wide effort to break up large and dysfunctional secondary schools into smaller and smarter ones (McDonald, 2014). Waterfront is one of those schools that actually did get smarter as well as smaller. That is, it taught itself to function differently from the big and dysfunctional middle school it helped replace. Its data use system is one manifestation of this. So is its distributed rather than hierarchical leadership. Today, it is harder at Waterfront than at most other secondary schools to distinguish easily between teachers and administrators. For example, in collaboration with the principal and assistant principal, full-time teachers lead the school's curriculum development, its technology management, its assessment planning, and its materials curating. The school also learned early to network with neighborhood organizations, including community health centers, youth centers, social service providers, and a nearby campus of the City University of New York. Together, the school and the neighborhood partners have built a thriving after-school program, and have managed to attract other significant financial and intellectual resources to benefit their students and the students' families.

Since its opening, according to our analysis of public online data available from the New York City Department of Education, the school has consistently served a student body that is more than 90% eligible for free lunch, between 15 and 35% English language learners, and 30 to 40% students with disabilities. Racially, the school's population has stayed roughly 65 to 75% Hispanic; 15 to 20% Black; 5% Asian; and 0 to 5% White. Although the school's passing rates (performance level 3 or 4) on statewide tests are well under the citywide averages in both English language arts (by 13 points), and math (by 29 points), the school outperforms its comparison group of schools in ELA. These are schools across the city that the district has matched with Waterfront for comparative purposes, based on similarities in students' incoming test scores, disability status, overage status, language needs, and economic needs. Meanwhile, Waterfront's record in advancing students' skill levels over the course of middle school is impressive. Most recently, all students at Waterfront who scored at level 2 on their 5th-grade literacy test or 5th-grade math test had by 8th-grade risen to levels 3 or 4. As for level 1-scoring 5th-graders, 55% had risen by 8th grade to 2, 3, or 4 in ELA, though only 13% had in math (New York City Department of Education, 2015–2016, online data).

At Waterfront, as at the other schools we studied, we followed Judith Warren Little's (2012) advice in studying data use in teaching to alternate *zooming out* and *zooming in*. The first involves articulating the school's theory of action with regard to data use in teaching: what the school aims to do and how, and then describing the plumbing the school has installed for the purpose. And the second involves illuminating what Little calls specific moments of data use when "teachers and others assign various meanings to data, make inferences from data, create explanations for observed patterns, and imagine useful responses to the patterns" (p. 160).

The account of the Waterfront data system that we present below is the result of much zooming out and in—for example, one day observing a school-wide meeting and interviewing the administrator who ran it, and the next day transcribing a teacher's moves from the perspectives of students he interacts with while teaching. Note, however, that the heart of the story we tell in this chapter is how the *out* and the *in* connect. Here, the plumbing runs all the way to what Richard Elmore (2008) calls the *instructional core* of the school.

ZOOMING OUT

In this first part of the deep dive, we compile what we know about the impact of implementing data use in teaching on the Waterfront School's macro-level systems. Our account relies especially on interviews and observations of the principal, the assistant principal, and two long-term and full-time teachers who also play significant leadership roles at the school. We focus here first on what we take to be the driving idea behind the school's implementation, and then on the learning community that makes this idea actionable. Finally, we explore a number of the school-wide routines and practices that implementation has spawned.

Driving Idea

Waterfront Principal Raquel Ortega (RO) introduced us to the school's driving idea with a pronouncement that at first puzzled us. "Task predicts performance," she said. Responding to our puzzled looks, she added that she believes what students *do* as they learn is the best predictor of what they *will* learn. We were still puzzled, so she continued, "This is why every task in a class needs to be aligned to a standard." Did she mean, we wondered, that teaching needs to mimic testing? No, we learned from further questioning, just the opposite. In RO's view, children are more likely to become genuinely engaged readers if their teacher asks them to read engaging books (rather than answer multiple choice questions about short passages that resemble ones found on standardized tests). The engaging task predicts an engaged performance.

Eventually, we tracked the phrase to Richard Elmore and his theory of the instructional core (City, Elmore, Fiarman, & Teitel, 2009, p. 30; Elmore, 2008). This is essentially what we have called in previous chapters the *wild triangle,* and what still other scholars of teaching have identified by other names (see, for example, Walter Doyle, 1983, and David Hawkins, 1974). Plainly put, Elmore and his colleagues argue that any improvement strategy for schooling has to deal with the content the teacher is teaching, their skillfulness in teaching it, and what the student is actually *doing* in response to the teaching. If the strategy is not purposefully designed to reach this core, they suggest, it amounts to nothing more than magical thinking. As RO put it, "You start with the standard, you create your instructional objective, and the objective itself is your assessment. That becomes the daily data collection"—accounting for what students actually *do* with reference to what you set out to help them do.

We finally understood. The flow of the data use system at Waterfront is engineered to go directly from standards to teaching, making the teaching standards-based from scratch, rather than retro-fitted once big-test data reports arrive. This makes the school less focused on deficit, and less likely to turn into what is called (disparagingly at Waterfront and else-where) "test prep."

One reason for this difference is that Waterfront has a lot of students with special needs, and big-test data often fails a validity check with respect to students with disabilities or English language learners (or both). Here is how teacher Jake Orfield (JO) described this check:

> Look, I have a set of 7th-graders where the average reading level is, maybe, 5th grade, with some outliers. So, no matter how much they may have an ability now to write about theme or setting, or find those things in texts they read, when they're thrown a [7th-grade-level standardized] test that they can't comprehend and they're spending all their energy decoding, they *can't* show [on this test] that they know this [other] stuff [even if they do].

JO's colleague, Lucas Nguyen (LN), made a similar point:

> We're extremely high-needs. The majority of our kids came in [to the 6th grade] not knowing how to capitalize, not punctuating, not indenting, having no idea what a paragraph is.

How does he know this, absent big-test data? Because he and his col-leagues ask their students right away in September to perform standards-focused reading, writing, speaking, and listening tasks. They embed the tasks within rich opening instructional units that interest the students and attune them to the achievement culture of the school. The units are devel-oped with a range of benchmarked development in mind from 3rd and 4th grade through 7th and 8th grade. And the teachers compile their own data on how the students perform these tasks, using Google spreadsheets that they share and discuss with each other.

An item analysis from the previous fall's big test that arrives later may tell JO that one of his students, Hector, missed a question intended to mea-sure Common Core Standard R3 (about analyzing the interactions among elements and features of a text), but JO likely knows this already. In any case, he would never (as happened in some other schools we studied) create worksheets on R3 based on big-test item analyses, and "regroup" Hector and other R3-deficient students to work on these worksheets. What he does instead is draw up learning plans for all his 7th-graders that embed R3 and provoke the students to *do* R3—that is, analyze text-based interactions. And he pulls and coaches students who fail to do it at the 6th-grade level, and also those who do it at higher levels. He wants to be assured that all his students are appropriately challenged by text and task. This is what it means to make teaching standards-based from scratch, and to make the learning task a performance assessment too.

Or LN may listen to Mirissa read aloud (assessing her comprehension, tracing her miscues, and even, at the end, submitting the results for standardized analysis online), but he may also pause Mirissa's reading to ask whether she knows why the text has suddenly stopped midline and skipped to the next line. And when she shakes her head no, LN may give this shift a name, "indent," and use a brief metaphor to explain it, involving perhaps the shifts a camera makes, or a piece of music. Then a few minutes later, at another "indent," he may explore with her the rationale for an indentation there, and how to incorporate the sound (and pause) into her read-aloud. And Mirissa may read it again with this inflection more obvious.

Of course, the quality of the teaching in such a system will only be as good as the standards it is anchored in, *and* as good as the teacher's facility in working with these standards across levels and content areas. The interest in the Common Core Standards among Waterfront staff preceded New York State's adoption of them. Here is LN's recollection on this point:

> The Common Core Standards had just been introduced—just the draft of them—when Raquel [RO] was like "We're doing this right away." And we [the rest of the faculty] were like "OK, let's do it." So, by the time New York had adopted Common Core, we were 2 years ahead. I mean we had already changed our rubrics to Common Core benchmarks and standards.

RO's enthusiasm (as well as her faculty's) for these standards were likely impelled by their sense that literacy and math achievement are crucial to their students' academic success, and that the emerging new standards seemed to cover the middle-school terrain of development in these areas with richness and authenticity. They wanted to teach themselves early and well how to navigate these new standards, not as a defense against assessment pressures, but as a spur to richer teaching. So while other schools in New York were worrying about tougher new standards, or complaining about them, this school told itself, in effect, "Let's put these to our own purpose," and there was a "we" in this pronouncement. In other words, the school's early adoption of the standards—even before official state adoption—and with strong faculty support—was a sign of what we called, in Chapter 5, action space. This is an arena for collective improvement work, marked by a commitment to mobilize capacity for the work from multiple sources, and the Common Core Standards were one source. Near the end of our study, however, New York State, like a number of other states, reexamined and changed its commitment to the Common Core Standards (see Chapter 3). But this will likely make little difference at Waterfront because the replacement standards in New York, called Next Generation Standards, are only superficially different, particularly when one considers the *tasks* they suggest (Harris, 2016; McDonald et al., 2016).

A Learning Community

Many other schools do not try to connect teaching to standards from scratch because they have too few teachers who are deeply knowledgeable in the content they teach. The problem can be acute in schools serving poverty-impacted communities (Duncan & Murnane, 2014; Jensen, 2009; Sutcher, Darling-Hammond, & Carver-Thomas, 2016). Waterfront is different because it managed to attract in its early years a critical mass of teachers with content and pedagogical content expertise—teachers like JO and LN—and it has managed to retain them. These teachers turned out to like the school's mission, its experimental attitude, its stable leadership, and the fact that it encourages teacher leadership. As LN told us, he was able at Waterfront to learn about administrative systems without becoming an administrator. When interviewed by Joseph McDonald (JM), JO made a similar point about learning data analysis without becoming a data specialist:

> *JO:* I am doing TC [TCRWP] running records with every student.
> *JM:* Every student in the school?
> *JO:* Yes. I have a period for that [in his daily schedule]. It's pretty interesting because I am getting a sense—you know it's rough—but you get a sense of grade level, you get a sense of fluency versus comprehension, and you can ascribe certain kinds of numbers to these. And you look at a test score—the student's daily score, or other data that might be there, and you can see divergences. What might be going on here with this student who is acing this reading thing [running record] and is clearly a high-level reader, but is getting 2s every year on the ELA test. What's happening there?

Each of JO's sentences here—about getting "a sense," ascribing numbers, seeing divergences, and even asking the question, "What's happening there?"—seem steeped in content knowledge (knowledge of the field) and pedagogical content knowledge (knowledge of how novices develop in a particular content field) (Shulman, 1987). On the other hand, not all Waterfront teachers are so deeply knowledgeable in these areas—or, indeed, in other areas. Much depends, JO told us, on their academic backgrounds, the duration of their careers to date, their skillfulness in classroom management, and what he called (after Carol Dweck, 2006) their "mindset." Without meaning to, he explained, some of his colleagues underestimate what their students can achieve. This shows up, he said, in the tasks they give them for learning. In cellular schools—with privacy norms governing teaching—variation in content expertise, in pedagogical expertise generally, and in mindset in particular, can prove disastrous for some students. But here again Waterfront Middle School is different. It is *not* cellular.

It is possible here for teachers to learn from each other, to share their own expertise and thus expand schoolwide expertise, even to influence each other's mindset. Indeed, the original Waterfront mission statement, JO told us, explicitly committed the school to being a learning community *for teachers* as well as students, and he told us, "We hew really closely to what that means." Many of the organizational routines and practices that we describe below derive from this commitment.

Routines and Practices

When we asked Principal RO in our initial interview what she would describe as special about the Waterfront Middle School with respect to its routines and practices, the first thing she told us was the way that the school taps external expertise. "We ground ourselves in a professional text," she said, "and then we work with it." This "work" uses seminars and text-based protocols to identify core ideas in the texts and possible applications of them to the school's work, and it involves efforts in content groups and grade-level teams to look together at student work with the text and possible applications of the text in mind. Over time, the school has let particular ideas from multiple texts (typically whole books, not just excerpts or articles) seep into the learning community. When RO told us, for example, that "task predicts performance," we discovered that she was channeling *Instructional Rounds in Education* (City et al., 2009). Other expert-authored texts that found their way into our Waterfront interview transcripts include those by David Allen (2013), Nancie Atwell (2015), Angela Duckworth (2016), Carol Dweck (2006), Anders Ericsson and Robert Pool (2016), Robert J. Marzano (2006, 2007), Anne Reeves (2011), Mark Seidenberg (2017), Paul Tough (2012, 2016), and Rick Wormeli (2006).

Nor is reading the only source of ideas for the school's learning community. The school regularly sends its most experienced teachers out to scout and learn from other schools or from external experts in varied fields (assessment, literacy, psychology, technology, and so on). In describing this phenomenon for us, LN drew an unusual picture (for a U.S. public school) of self-direction in professional learning:

> Raquel [RO] is absolutely supportive of any sort of professional development endeavors that we undertake. Anytime I need to go on a PD, I just tell her where I'm going and when, and there's no questions asked. The trust is there, and the assumption of both your professionalism as well as your competence. It's the very opposite of what's happening nationally in terms of the discourse on teaching, right?—the assumption that teachers are just not very, I don't know, *self-driven*, or not the smartest people.

Meanwhile, the school's more experienced teachers—in addition to curating materials, managing technology, and leading curriculum development and assessment—also mentor the less experienced ones. So what they learn spreads quickly throughout the learning community.

The next "special" thing about Waterfront that RO mentioned was faculty inter-visitation, a derivative of *Instructional Rounds* (City et al., 2009), Nell Panero and Joan Talbert's (2013) work on low-inference transcription, and other sources. In a fascinating double entendre, the Waterfront faculty calls this inter-visitation "IV." Indeed, it aims to inject the learning community into every teacher's practice. On a quarterly basis, each teacher in the school is paired with another teacher—typically one who teaches some of the same students—and the IV partners observe each other's teaching once a week. The teachers have all been trained to make low-inference transcriptions of what they observe, and they swap these and discuss them in a planned weekly meeting. LN told us that these meetings used to be privately scheduled by the partners, but under that arrangement, their quality varied widely. So, the school decided to hold the meetings simultaneously during common planning time, and to hire an outside consultant to help facilitate them—to set a tone, to rehearse the protocol occasionally, and to ensure generally that the pairs' conversations remain data-focused, undefensive, and honest.

We asked the "What's special?" question of our other informants too. Assistant Principal Joshua Barnes (JB) called attention to the school's use of technology—not just to manage data but to create it. In Chapter 2, we used a brief account of this practice to ground our discussion of some essential moves of teaching. The practice involves a teacher's tracking a student discussion by simultaneously typing it into a Google Doc. LN, who is one of the Waterfront teachers who engages in this practice, told us that his students with special needs benefit greatly from "seeing what they're saying. It *validates* what they say." LN was also deeply involved in the launch of another Google-inspired practice, this time with Google Sheets rather than Docs. Note that the school was an early adopter of G Suite (Google for schools). He told us the following story as yet another special thing about the school:

> It started off as a sort of behavior system. We had a really toxic group [in the second year of the school's existence], our 8th-grade group. They were unruly, and there were no systems really. And so I came in and was like, "What *is* this?" I mean, I'm not the nicest teacher, I'm a strict teacher, so I proposed several things. I created a bathroom pass system and a productivity tracking system where students give themselves a 1 through 5 each day on a rubric based on how productive they were, how much they contributed to the classroom discussion and classroom environment, and things like that. [He points to chart paper on the

wall that outlines five different levels of productivity]. And so we [he and colleagues then teaching 8th-graders] used that. And we had some external motivators like a pizza party or something for us to get the kids to buy in. And this worked. I mean that class became much easier to manage, much calmer, but it was still a hard class.

Then this sort of expanded. Orfield [JO] was doing what we call "status of the class," where he was tracking attendance and page numbers [how many pages students managed to read during independent reading]. I was tracking attendance as well, but he was putting [these various data elements] into one Google spreadsheet, and so we merged my system with his system, and then another teacher really wanted to track—in almost real time—[students' achievement of] the [recently introduced] Common Core Standards. In many ways, it was an amalgam of our work together—the priorities for me and for Jake [JO] and for the other teacher—and it just became this *thing*.

JM asked, "What thing?" And LN opened his computer and scrolled through a long series of Google Sheets. They contained not only LN's data use in teaching, but his colleagues' too. LN manages the integrated sheets for the school. "You'll see it throughout different classes in different iterations," he told us, "but for the most part it's the same. It's *everything*"—that is, everything that he and/or his colleagues want to track in a systematic way. In many cases, however, the actual trackers are the students themselves. "The kids keep track of the types of books [they read in independent reading], the number of pages that they read, as well as the number of books they read."

Of course, LN's Google Sheets include big-test data as well as intimate data, and while he focuses on the standards and the intimate data that measure students' progress in achieving them, he also tracks the big-data impact, as he illustrates in the next transcript excerpt. LN is not anti–big test. He is pro-multiple-forms-of-assessment, so long as the data they all yield is ultimately owned by students themselves.

Last year, one kid came into [my] 6th grade [class] with a 4 in their [5th-grade] ELA test, [but] six kids left with a 4, and several of them were 2s and became 4s. My kids are definitely looking at their own growth, setting their own goals, and talking about really deliberate things that they can do to improve their growth. They do reflections, they take it home, and there's always an ongoing conversation about growth. It's always about growth.

Then LN talked about Wilson, who might be considered one of his student mentors, whose growth by means of self-monitoring proved LN's faith in the strategy:

So, one of my students last year, Wilson, wanted to be like a Blood, and was following all the [neighborhood] bad boys—quote/unquote "bad boys." But at the same time, he was really deliberate about his work. He totally bought into [my] brainwashing [about the value of closely monitoring one's own reading], and ended up getting a 4 on his [state] ELA test. And guess what he is now? He doesn't leave his classroom, he does all the right things. Every time I see him, I'm like, are you still on the road to whatever high school you want? And being a Blood is not even part of who he is, so it's changed his entire outlook on who he is as a person and also who he potentially can be.

And talking about Wilson led LN back to data use in teaching.

You know, when *Data Wise* [Boudett et al., first edition, 2007] [came out], and data systems were being pushed into the schools [by the New York City Department of Education], it was like, "Okay, just keep data." Really, that was all it was [that is, a plug-in model]. As opposed to how can data be a more iterative process, and you're able to see bigger, systematic things going on, but then filter it out so you can use it, and the kids can use it. I think that's the hardest thing to do is to get the kids to use that data.

Meanwhile, because LN and his colleagues merge their Google Sheets, they can visit each other's data use. They can see what others track that they do not, and they can research one of their own student's reading or writing growth in the context of another teacher's classroom. LN told us that he and his colleagues use the sheets in talking with parents, in talking with each other about students' progress, and in talking with students themselves. Note, however, that while the faculty is organized as a learning community, it is also empowered to innovate. So, RO told us, no teacher has to track what others track beyond certain basics like attendance and reading growth.

ZOOMING IN

In Chapter 2, we described three continually shifting dynamics underlying teaching, identified by David Cohen (2011). They involve what to teach, how to engage students' cooperation in learning it, and how to figure out what the students understand. In the same chapter, we described how teachers manage these dynamics with a repertoire of behaviors, including four in particular. We call them *pressing*, *pulling*, *asking*, and *walking away*. In this section, we use these behaviors to frame scenes from LN's teaching.

In one of our early interviews of LN, he oriented us to his classroom.

One thing you'll notice is that it's very consistent. It's very stable, and it's very predictable. Because of the population of kids I have, I feel like making the classroom, all the structural things . . . [interrupts himself] . . . I mean if you ask a kid where a pencil sharpener is, they can find it for you, or where the scissors are, they can find it for you. It's just very easy for them in terms of the transitions, especially coming from an elementary school to a middle school setting.

His classroom is predictable too in its scheduling, typically beginning with 30 minutes of independent reading, followed by 60 minutes of interactive work combining reading, writing, speaking, and listening.

Independent Reading

For independent reading, LN's students read books they have selected from an extensive classroom library of young-adult books, both fiction and non-fiction—all identified by Fountas and Pinnell (2016) levels of text complexity, all previously read closely by LN himself. He continually searches for and is often successful in finding new funding to buy more books, and he spends spare hours reading book reviews, thinking about good matches between books and kids. When students enter LN's classroom at the start of class, most of them immediately take out their books (previously drawn from the classroom library) as well as their journals (in which they make notes about their reading). Then they start reading. LN uses this part of the class as a time to conference privately with individual students and take stock of their text engagement and comprehension, though in doing this he is careful not to take up too much of a reader's reading time or to disturb other readers.

In depicting both this first part of LN's typical classroom teaching, and also the later part, we draw on an observation by Dana Karin (DK) on a November morning. LN was teaching a class of 6th-graders. DK transcribed what she saw and heard in a low-inference way, tracking not just LN's moves and words, but those of a convenient sample of students close at hand, four girls whom LN had asked her to sit with at table 4. We call them here S1–S4. In our account of the morning below, we combine DK's low-inference notes with post-observation interpretation, enhanced by LN's reading of the notes and response to them later the same day.

S1 and S3 begin reading immediately, while S2 glances around the room. She rubs her eyes and glances at her fingernails. S4 is slow to take her book and journal out of her bag.

S1 holds a hand on her forehead over her eyes, and occasionally rubs her eyes. She holds her book vertically on the table. S2 holds her book in her hands, and rests her head on her right fist. S4 is chewing on something, and has the book flat in front of her on the table. LN comes up beside her, and gestures toward her journal—a reminder to keep track of her reading.

S1, S2, and S3 all continue reading as before. S4 is still reading with the book flat on the table, but now she covers her mouth with her sweatshirt. Then she begins fidgeting, and turning in her chair. Next, she lifts the book off the table and continues reading with the book in her hands, and her elbows resting on the table. Meanwhile, LN walks to different parts of the room, and conferences quickly and quietly with several students. Then he walks toward S1, writes on a paper and slides it to her. She glances at the paper, then returns to reading.

"All right," LN says at the end of roughly 28 minutes of independent reading, "Give yourselves 30 seconds more." Then he touches the computer, and a spreadsheet opens on the screen. With time up, he asks all students to respond quickly with two numbers when he calls their names from the spreadsheet. First is the number of pages they have just read, and second is either 1 or 0 depending on whether they made it or not into "the zone." The term comes from a 2007 book by Nancie Atwell, and refers to a kind of text engagement that makes a reader relatively impervious to distraction. There is no penalty for students who assign themselves a 0 rather than a 1 on a given day, but the record over time of 0s and 1s, committed to a student-specific Google Sheet, becomes a powerful data input for LN's sense of his students' reading facility, and for the students' own sense of progress in reading development.

LN is a fast typist, and this zone reporting process moves quickly. Reflecting later on this part of DK's original transcript, LN explained:

> While this [both the page numbers and the zone score] is purely self-assessed [that is, by the students], I do sometimes [privately] challenge students on whether they were *actually* in the zone—particularly when I notice them not really engaged in the text throughout the independent reading session.

This is one way that he combines pressing and walking away. In effect, he tells the students that they will always pick the page number and zone scores themselves, but that he always reserves the right to be their alert and honest coach. And it is the coach who advises them in private pulling sessions about the kind and level of book they might try next and why. "About half the students," he told DK, "are reading books that were co-selected by me"—a crucial, under-the-radar part of his pedagogy.

Self-Assessing Their Writing

According to DK's transcript, LN transitions crisply to the second part of the block, focused this time on writing about their writing:

> Put your independent reading books away. Just your writing journal stays out. Because otherwise you have too much stuff. [Pause, surveying the room quickly] Table 1 is ready.
>
> Remember, we've been giving each other feedback [on the first draft of an essay]. Today you're going to use the rubric [that the students themselves helped devise] to give yourselves a grade.

He tells them also that they are about to see for the first time the grade that an anonymous peer using the same rubric gave this first draft, plus comments that LN himself made on the draft. "You will have until Friday," he adds, "to revise." But today, he adds, "You're going to write a note to yourself about what you *need* to revise."

DK's transcription at this point notes that Students 1–4 all look at the screen as LN calls attention to the specific steps and durations of the work coming up. Meanwhile, he walks about the room and distributes materials to each table, laying the materials face down. Students wait to turn them over until he gives the signal.

This multiday assignment reflects what Principal RO described as the Waterfront School's commitment to orient teaching to standards-based tasks. At the same time, the assignment is complex—in fact, sophisticated. LN uses two standards rather than one. The first, in the language of the Common Core Standards, is "Write arguments to support claims with clear reasons and relevant evidence." And the second is "Draw evidence from literary or informational texts to support analysis, reflection, and research" (CCSS ELA-Literacy.w.6.1, and CCSS.ELA-Literacy.w.6.9 [www.corestandards.org/ELA-Literacy]). Thus, LN links the writing to the students' independent reading (which includes both literary and informational texts). They must construct and support a claim with relevant evidence drawn from four texts they have recently read.

The kind of elaboration of standards-based teaching evident in this 6th-grade assignment depends mightily on content knowledge. The teacher not only has to have a good sense of the standards, but also a good sense of how they might mix and match, and of how reading and writing really work and how young readers and writers can connect them. Meanwhile, the rubric—which LN refers to at one point as a "simple checklist"—is his students' principal guide to form, and it is rather loose in form, deliberately so. There is no forced writing design in this assignment—for example, a "five-paragraph essay," or a direction to the students to state their claim in the opening sentence, then devote one paragraph each to a relevant piece of evidence. Forced designs can be helpful to young writers, though only so long as they are needed as training wheels. Sadly, however, they often stay on the bikes too long.

The writing task that LN assigns here is related to the 6th-grade big test that these students will take the following spring, but the assignment is *not* lifted straight from a previous version of the test, and its form is quite different. The big test asks students to write "extended responses" to *given* passages of text, based on *given* prompts. This is a kind of writing peculiar to big-test taking. Even the name, "extended response," is inauthentic with respect to real-world writing, and LN would likely never use this name except to describe the test. He understands that writing, beyond the mundane, is about constructing the right form for a set of ideas that one has conjured up on one's own. He wants his students to experience this—hard as it is to experience. Task predicts performance. Still, he understands that 12-year-olds need strong scaffolding for this constructive work, and he arranges for this—first, at the front end of this assignment when he worked with them to turn what he calls "the Common Core grown-up language" into "language we understand," and then through several sessions of peer- and self-assessment punctuated by pulling and pressing.

Meanwhile, the "checklist" reminds them—though not in so many words—about the need to stake a claim, about the fact that some claims need subclaims, about the fact that all claims require evidence to make them credible (in this case, specific and relevant references to the four texts). And LN also tosses in a special challenge that his students seem to enjoy, even over-enjoy: Can they create an "engaging hook" for their essay?

What Happens at Table 4

Table 4 is where Students 1, 2, 3, and 4 sit, along with DK, who is observing the teaching partly through their experiences. And it is improvisatory teaching. One of the problems with ordinary conceptions of data use in teaching, particularly on the part of policymakers, is that it often fails to account for the improvisatory dimension of teaching, when teachers respond on the spot to quick cues from students, content, and situational circumstances. Here, we follow LN's improvisations—in pressing, pulling, asking, and walking away—through the experiences of students 1–4. Of course, LN must work the whole room, not just table 4, so our account below distorts the complexity. However, it makes the dynamics within the complexity more visible.

Note that as LN works, all his students have their *own* work, and the work is *not* worksheets. It's writer's work. They all have before them a first draft of an essay that they have a stake in, and they have feedback to consider on this draft from both a peer and their teacher. They are expected to review this feedback now, and evaluate the draft themselves from the perspective of a reader. They have deadline pressures. Moreover, LN has pushed them to engage in their own improvisation: "Pretend that you're not you—that you're the reader [not the writer]. Can you find the claim?"

S1 gets to work right away on reading the critical input on her draft. She reads it aloud but quietly. When LN walks by the table, she asks him if she can draw arrows on the material she has received, and he encourages her to do this, then he walks away. The next time he comes by, he pulls her out of her reading to inquire into her understanding of inference and critique—terms he has deliberately taught and used many times. She seems a little puzzled by the terms, but he just points to the checklist box labeled "inferential and critical," and says, "You look and make the decision." Then he walks away again. A few minutes later, she puts a checkmark in this box.

S2 has been rapidly checking off boxes, and is now beginning her note to self. Glancing down at what she is writing, LN says, "I like that you're doing it in an impersonal way." Then he asks, "Is everything in terms of the evidence fine? Do you have direct quotes or summaries?" She answers promptly, "Mm hmm."

S3 initiates the first contact with LN by calling him over. She tells him that he has given her the wrong essay, and he quickly makes the switch to the right one. Later, he initiates a contact—a pull he might have preplanned. "Remember the chart where you went from the general to specific?" he asks her, and he helps her find the chart in her writing journal. Then he coaches her to think about how she might make her claim in this essay more general—to move from the four books she has cited "to more people, to learn their lessons."

"To connect to the reader?" she asks him, using what seems a stock phrase she has heard. LN presses beyond the phrase, "How can your claim apply to people in the whole world?" She responds by using another stock phrase, "Connect to life lessons?"

He ignores the question, and asks simply, "Does your claim speak only to these four books? Or could it be bigger?" She answers, "It could be bigger."

He asks, "What are you writing about?" She answers, "The characters." Expanding the context, he asks, "Where else can you find characters?" She replies, "In the paragraphs." And he tells her that she is still stuck in the four books. He adds, "Can you make this claim more general and apply it to other people?" "Yes," she tells him, and he walks away.

When LN next returns to table 4, S3 has redrafted the claim. "Is this better?" she asks. "Hmm," he replies. Then, in an unusual feat of pressing past initial success, he declines to affirm it, and instead presses further: "There are actually two claims here," he says, then walks away.

At the start of this activity, S4 plays with her hair. Then she picks up her pencil, but puts it down promptly. Next, she stands up, walks to the front board, then returns to her seat. When she sits down, LN is there.

"Is this my grade?" she asks him, referring to the peer's grade. "No," he answers, and tells her that this anonymous reviewer has advised her about how to improve her writing on the next draft. Then he presses her on how she expresses her claim: "Stories teach readers that they can expect ups and downs. Isn't that your claim? But can you think of some ups and downs? This is not specific enough."

Again, S4 walks away, this time to the back of the room. Then she returns to her chair and rubs her head.

When the allotted time for this activity expires, LN does a wrap—one that incorporates yet another press, even as it also demonstrates appreciation of progress: "Some of you are too involved in your hook. Is your essay about *your hook*? Some of you have questions about the relevance of your evidence. We're in different places, but [collectively] we're in a really good place, and *you* are in a good place."

Earlier in this chapter, we quoted LN describing himself as "not a nice teacher." He meant, we think, that he presses his students incessantly; sometimes to the point of brusqueness, though always with their interests in mind, especially their growth as readers and writers. And he makes space and time for this growth to happen—for example, by walking away while they think, or tolerating when *they* walk away in order to think or gain composure for thinking. He also makes thinking visible, and, indeed, making thinking visible, more than anything else, is what he means by data (Krechevsky et al., 2013; Ritchart et al., 2011). He makes thinking visible, for example, whenever he asks students to exchange their work for peer review, whenever he records their speech on the spot in a Google Doc, and at the end of every class when he asks them to call out a productivity score.

"Now, as you're cleaning up," he said with minutes to spare on this occasion, "I'm going to call out your name and you'll give me your productivity score for the day." And, as they did before with respect to reading, the students rated themselves aloud, and LN recorded the ratings in a Google Sheet on the screen.

Later—as he told us he nearly always manages to do—LN likely found a few moments after school to look over the zone scores and the productivity scores, and to jot down any insights he had gleaned this morning from this data or from his many interactions and observations, whether about the learning or the teaching.

Focus on Data

Over the years, LN, a data enthusiast, has worked to simplify the data he manages, and to incorporate his students into the management. This is the data he draws on as he presses, pulls, asks, and walks away. "I've tried to shed a lot of the extraneous data," he told us, "to really get at data that I can use to help students make certain choices about their learning." As he spoke, he pulled up his master data table on his laptop, and proceeded to describe it to us, column by column:

1. Engagement in independent reading (in the zone or not). Students track themselves.
2. Number of pages read daily ("and at this time of the year, they're reading massive amounts"). Students track themselves.
3. Reading levels in terms of text complexity. LN tracks this based on his monitoring of independent reading, as checked periodically by running records. The school uses the TCRWP Running Record Assessment system.
4. Latest big-test scores. Available from the State.
5. Homework. LN tracks this, he tells us, "Because parents care but I don't."
6. Daily productivity scores. Students track themselves.
7. Students' reading goals. Students formulate these themselves, with input from LN.

Note that big-test data gets only one spot on this list (4), and standardized assessment data (big-test or intimate) only two spots (3 and 4). Note also that students themselves are the data sources for four other spots. The combination is a refreshing variation on what schools classically call "classroom grading," which is typically focused on products and deadlines rather than on processes and progress in reaching competency targets. Indeed, when LN comments that he collects data on homework "because parents care but I don't," he is referring obliquely to this classic system, and in the process suggesting that he both respects the role that homework plays in parents' monitoring of their children's engagement, and also focuses himself on richer measures of growth. Finally, note that four of the seven spots on LN's list concern reading. He emphasizes reading over writing (and listening and speaking) because he trusts more in reading as a driver for his students' overall literacy development. However, he also understands that this driving works only to the extent that he makes it work. Thus, in the second 60-minute part of each class session, he connects reading, writing, listening, and speaking; and he is a skillful coach across these areas. Still, the *first* thing he pushes for, he told us, is good reading choices, ones that will build stamina, fluency, and a love of reading. This is part of the "brainwashing" he mentioned above in talking about his student, Wilson—the one who no longer aspires to be a Blood.

SUMMING UP

In this final deep dive, we explore a case of implementation of the innovation called data use in teaching. Systems throughout this middle school have been deeply affected—changing how teaching is designed, how the school is managed, how teachers are mentored, how they relate to one another, what kinds of data matter most to them, how teachers teach, and how students learn. The implementation here seems less the consequence of driving external forces, than of a pervasive—perhaps contagious—willingness within this school to let go of previous conceptions in all these areas, to experiment with new directions, and to share data from these experiments. Meanwhile, the story of what happened at Waterfront Middle School picks up on the theme, suggested earlier in the book, namely that data use in teaching might be better thought of as data use in learning.

Expanding Time and Space for Learning

In the introduction to her 2011 book, *Where Great Teaching Begins*, Anne Reeves warns that it is not tenable, at a time when all children are expected to learn difficult things at high levels, to think about teaching as only what teachers plan and do. This conception of teaching, she writes, must be expanded to include what students plan and do. Note that she is not just saying here—as countless other reformers have—that in the face of new expectations, our conceptions of *learning* or of *assessing* have to change. She says that *teaching* must change, too, and in a certain way. It is as if she were shouting, "Give the kids the keys! You know they can't learn to drive without driving."

We think of the change she proposes in physical terms—namely as adjustments in the way teaching typically uses time and space. The adjustments alter things like "all-eyes-on-me," teacher-show-and-tell, teacher-centric "discussions" that search mostly for "right" answers, and desk-bound worksheets. They replace changing daily agendas (also known as lesson plans) with stable routines like independent reading time, project-based team time, writing time, "critical circles," and so on. And in the process, time is *gained* from the predictability of how time is spent. The adjustments alter space to incorporate classroom libraries, project tables, meeting carpets, display space, rehearsal space, and so on. Depending on educational level, teaching and learning space may be expanded beyond the classroom box to hallway cubicles and benches, studios, labs, library, the outdoors, fieldwork, and community internships. One point of all these adjustments is to make student learning more visible, more revisable, more available for teacher, peer, and mentor coaching. And another is to lend it more means of expression—including especially sound, touch, and movement.

In these physically adjusted settings, students control more of the projects they work on, they work more with each other, they rehearse things, they move about the classroom and the school, and they document and display their work. They also have time and space to work privately as needed, and their teacher asks them more questions privately, ones that are not pre-planned, ones that focus more directly on work at hand and the problems that students themselves identify. The teacher does more teaching on the spot, and also more "walking away"—that is, refraining from interference, encouraging the kind of confusion that can lead to new insight. In these settings, work products themselves become data for teaching and learning.

Exemplary Systems

If you are a classroom teacher, expanding time and space for learning is probably not something you should try on your own. It's something, however, that you should encourage in your school, and search for if you change schools. All the exemplars of this New Direction that we cite are systems for organizing whole schools, and these systems are typically supported by networks, as well as by network-based coaches and materials. Some have deep roots that contribute enormous practical histories. These include, for example, two long-term contributors to international schooling from Italy: the Reggio Emilia system (see www.reggiochildren.it; also Gandini, Hill, Cadwell, & Schwall, 2015; and Krechevsky et al., 2013); and the Montessori system (see American Montessori Society, 2018.). Another deep-rooted system, from Germany, is Waldorf schooling (see Oppenheimer, 1999). With their own spins on what it means, all three do what Anne Reeves calls for: incorporate what students plan and do into what teachers plan and do.

Other exemplars of this New Direction are products of late 20th-century and early 21st-century school reform. One of these is EL schooling, which we explored in the New Direction following Chapter 5. Others include Big Picture Learning, an international network whose mantra is "one student at a time" that substitutes rich advisory systems and internships for courses and classes (see McDonald, Klein & Riordan, 2009); HTH, a network of charter schools in southern California that takes project-based learning to exquisite heights (see High Tech High, 2018); and Harvard Project Zero (see www.pz.harvard.edu) which has been researching and advocating for this new direction across the world for more than 50 years.

Major Findings: The Reader's Interpretive Turn

The research described in this book was conducted in nine schools, all of them in New York City. Given the small sample and the particular context, the findings are limited in a strict sense to only these schools. Still, small-scale but intensive studies like ours can have resonant value well beyond their settings. This depends a great deal, however, on researchers striking a bargain with their readers. We hope it is one we have managed to strike with you. Throughout the book, we have tried to make what we observed and experienced in our research as clear and as vivid as possible. But now it is your interpretive turn. You must reflect on our observations and experiences by the light of your needs and interests. How are the schools and systems we studied like and unlike the ones that concern you? How do our findings seem applicable—albeit by transference—to situations you care about and must act on? How might you test out these findings in your different settings?

To help you consider these questions, we end by listing what we take to be our five major findings—the ones with the greatest local validity, and highest potential transfer value. Of course, you have seen these findings before, scattered across the book, and perhaps at times rendered too subtly, or worn thin by repetition. In what follows, we thicken them. For emphasis, we use imperative verbs in naming them, but we intend the fullest respect for your discretion in taking their cues.

Respect Complexity

Data use in teaching is a complex innovation for a complex system. It involves design and implementation at multiple levels—legislative and policy levels, districts, schools, classrooms, even relationships among teachers and students. Yet some champions of the innovation at all these levels wish away these complexities. They pretend that the innovation is simpler, that it is installable without customization, that it is magic. Implicitly, they deny the complexities of schooling itself, and in the process they threaten the impact of what they champion.

Expect Disruption

Data use in teaching is a disruptive agent, though it can be a beneficial one too. It aims to help all students learn more deeply, by changing deep patterns in learning and teaching. And deep patterns resist change. Moreover, because the innovation has come from far away, through layers of advocacy, distortion, banal misinterpretation, and inadvertent slippage, it can arrive in a school or a classroom looking dangerous. Whoever greets it first—typically a district or school leader—must negotiate its entry, initiate the reframing of its argument to suit the new context, then invite other colleagues to do the same at other levels of the system. Absent this serial, interpretive reframing, the innovation will either be sloughed off or fought off.

Focus on the Triangle

Data is not the heart of data use in teaching. Learning is. And learning in school depends ultimately on learners' engagement with content, on the meaningfulness they discern in the content, and on the knowledge and skillfulness of the teachers who guide their encounters with the content. All that data can do is manage to penetrate this wild triangle, then inform operations there. How well it does this depends first on whether schools understand that this is what must happen—understand that data use in teaching is a challenge, not a magic act. It depends too on whether the school is organized to route data in this way, whether it distributes authority for interpreting data and inventing ways to use it thoughtfully inside the triangle, and whether it develops a collective sense of what this looks like and feels like.

Expand Resources

Successful implementation of data use in teaching requires securing and aligning new resources to support the implementation at multiple levels. They include money, materials, talent, and ideas. There is nothing easy about growing such resources, though even in deeply poverty-impacted schools, it is possible. Success depends especially on cultivating ownership by a *we* that suffuses not only a school's leadership team, but its teachers, staff, outside consultants, and those the school must answer to, namely district officials and parents. The most successful of the schools we studied created and sustained teacher learning communities, and thereby expanded teachers' facility with data production and data analysis; increased teachers' content knowledge; and curated what might otherwise have been a bewildering array of available materials to support data use in teaching. Meanwhile, the expansion of human and intellectual resources in these schools contributed to the expansion of financial resources too, typically by generating a sense of progress throughout and eventually beyond the school community—first fostering trust, then reputation.

Serve the Primary Stakeholders

In the most successful of the schools we studied, data use by teachers became data use by learners, offering students greater opportunities to understand, monitor, and report on their own learning needs and learning gains. In the process, this disruptive innovation uprooted students' own deeply ingrained ideas of what teaching and schooling *can do*. They *can* serve a learner's interest. They *can* change a mindset. They *can* change a life.

Our Own Data (and Data Use)

Following guidance from the Spencer Foundation, which supported our research, and in collaboration with the Research Alliance for New York City Schools, we recruited nine New York City schools (five elementary and four middle) to join us as participants in this project. We recruited them first based on their status as poverty-impacted schools, and then on their reputations as active data users among the networks that supported them.

In each of our nine schools, with guidance from the principal, we recruited a "focal teacher" to serve as a key ground-level data source for insight into teaching with data, and also as a key guide to the school's internal system of organizing itself to support such practice. All the focal teachers taught at either the 4th-grade level or the 7th-grade level (though some of the 7th-grade teachers taught 6th-graders too, and we studied them in that context as well). The middle-school teachers were all English teachers. And we observed elementary-school teachers only in the context of their teaching literacy. Thus, the data use we explore in this book is data use in teaching literacy. Our rationale for this limitation was that *what* is taught always matters in teaching and must be attended to in studying it, and that keeping this *what* consistent across research sites might help us better understand the sites and better communicate this understanding. Although we acknowledge that teaching literacy differs in significant ways from teaching other subjects, we trust our readers to engage in what Chris Argyris and Donald Schön (1996) call reflective transfer, which we regard as the bedrock of validity in qualitative research. In our case, this means thoughtfully transferring our findings from the particularities of poverty-impacted New York City schools to the particularities of other contexts of interest, and also from the particularities of teaching literacy to the particularities of teaching other subjects.

Over 2 or 3 years (depending on site), we observed our focal teachers' teaching on numerous occasions, and prepared low-inference transcriptions of these observations (Panero & Talbert, 2013). We typically transcribed not only the teacher's words and actions, but those of a small convenient sample of their students—convenient because they were sitting and working near us. The transcriptions became the basis of follow-up conversations with the teachers—often immediately after an observation, or sometimes shortly after one, and sometimes online rather than in-person. We typically began these conversations by asking the teachers what they may have meant by a certain phrase or a certain move captured in the transcription, and also what they may have been thinking at that moment about a particular student's thoughts, actions, and learning history. Of course, the teachers understood our interest in the connection between data and teaching, so they often called attention to it as the conversation proceeded. But we seldom pressed for this, asking them instead to simply invite us into their teaching practices.

Mindful of one of the major recommendations that emerged from the Spencer-sponsored *American Journal of Education* and *Teachers College Record* volumes, we also investigated the organizational systems of the schools and the routines and deep behaviors that characterize these systems. We observed team meetings and "data meetings," and interviewed the educators who facilitated these (Spillane, 2012, 2014). Of course, we also interviewed school leaders including principals and assistant principals.

We transcribed all these data records, and stored them in an electronic database management system, *Dedoose*, and we used the functionalities of *Dedoose* to code the content of the records based on our original as well as our emerging research questions. Initially we used 13 codes. Examples include references to *organizational routines* involved in data use in teaching—1,487 (the highest count), out of 9,118 code applications; 1,361 references to *kinds of data*; 1,129 references to *student performance data;* and 1,004 references to *educational policy.* Note that these numbers refer to applications of code—with 2 and sometimes 3 coders across the 90 transcripts. Nearly all of our 13 codes also had subcodes, helping us delve below the surface of data use in teaching; for example, under *policy*, references *to special education* or *standardized testing.*

Once we had completed this first round of coding, we also used *Dedoose* to track our emerging findings by means of analytic memos. Members of the research team read through the coded transcripts and wrote memos tied to specific coded excerpts. This process produced 302 memos, and we coded these using a fresh set of codes influenced by what we had learned from the earlier stage of analysis. At the top of the memo coding count were references to *teaching* (147), all linked to excerpts in which research participants explicitly spoke about teaching.

The coding and memo-writing involved four members of the research team (the three authors and Susan Neuman), and it was guided by continual efforts via meetings and shared PowerPoint presentations to ensure common cross-team understanding of codes, themes, and emerging findings.

In the end, our interviewing and observation produced 90 transcripts, ranging from 2,965 to 141,843 words each, with a median of 23,148. The volume of our data follows Catherine Riessman's (2008) advice to preserve the narrative structures of what research participants say, and to avoid simply extracting the "content" of their narratives as initially perceived. And it has enabled us in this book to heed Sara Lawrence-Lightfoot and Jessica Hoffmann Davis's (1997) call for research-based writing that goes beyond mere reporting of context, detail, and theme, and uses imagery, symbol, dialogue, and aesthetic composition to convey meaning indirectly. What we call our deep dives are portraits in the Lawrence-Lightfoot and Davis tradition.

References

Allen, D. (2013). *Powerful teacher learning: What the theatre arts teach about collaboration.* Lanham, MD: Rowman & Littlefield.

Allen, D., & Blythe, T. (2004). *The facilitator's book of questions: Tools for looking together at student and teacher work.* New York, NY: Teachers College Press.

American Montessori Society. (2018). *Introduction to Montessori method.* Retrieved from www.amshq.org/Montessori-Education/Introduction-to-Montessori/

Argyris, C., & Schön, D. A. (1996). *Organizational learning II: Theory, method, and practice.* Reading, MA: Addison-Wesley.

Atwell, N. (2007). *The reading zone: How to help kids become skilled, passionate, habitual, critical readers.* New York, NY: Scholastic.

Atwell, N. (2015). *In the middle: A lifetime of learning about writing, reading, and adolescents* (3rd ed.). Portsmouth, NH: Heinemann.

Ayers, W. (2010). *To teach: The journey of a teacher* (3rd ed.). New York, NY: Teachers College Press.

Ayers, W., & Alexander-Tanner, R. (2010). *To teach: The journey in comics.* New York, NY: Teachers College Press.

Beadie, N. (2016). The federal role in education and the rise of social science research: Historical and comparative perspectives. In P. A. Alexander, F. J. Levine, & W. F. Tate, (Eds.), *Review of Research in Education, Vol. 40. Education research: A century of discovery* (pp. 1–37). Washington, DC: AERA.

Berger, R., Rugen, L., & Woodfin, L. (2014). *Leaders of their own learning.* San Francisco, CA: Jossey-Bass.

Blythe, T., Allen, D., & Powell, B. S. (2015*). Looking together at student work* (3rd ed.). New York, NY: Teachers College Press.

Bogart, A., & Landau, T. (2005). *The viewpoints book: A practical guide to viewpoints and composition.* New York, NY: Theatre Communications Group.

Bolman, L. G., & Deal, T. E. (1997). *Reframing organizations: Artistry, choice, and leadership* (2nd ed.). San Francisco, CA: Jossey-Bass.

Boudett, K. P., City, E. A., & Murnane, R. J. (2013). *Data wise: A step-by-step guide to using assessment results to improve teaching and learning* (revised and expanded ed.). Cambridge, MA: Harvard Education Press. [Also cited: 1st ed., 2007].

Breidenstein, A., Fahey, K., Glickman, C., & Hensley, F. (2012). *Leading for powerful learning: A guide for instructional leaders.* New York, NY: Teachers College Press.

Brown, J. S., & Duguid, P. (2000). *The social life of information.* Boston. MA: Harvard Business School Press.

Brown, P., & Rans, R. (1984). Material girl [Recorded by Madonna]. On *Like a virgin* [LP]. New York, NY: Sire Records.

Bryk, A. S., Easton, J. Q., Kerbow, D., Rollow, S. G., & Sebring, P. A. (1993). *A view from the elementary schools: The state of reform in Chicago*. Chicago, IL: Consortium on Chicago School Research, University of Chicago.

Bryk, A. S., Gomez, L. M., Grunow, A., & LeMahieu, P. (2015). *Learning to improve: How America's schools can get better at getting better*. Cambridge, MA: Harvard Education Press.

Bryk, A. S., Sebring, P. B., Allensworth, E., Lupescu, S., & Easton, J. Q. (2010). *Organizing schools for improvement: Lessons from Chicago*. Chicago, IL: University of Chicago Press.

Cervone, B. (2007). When reach exceeds grasp: Taking the Annenberg Challenge to scale. In R. Bachetti & T. Ehrlich (Eds.), *Reconnecting education and foundations: Turning good intentions into educational capital* (pp. 139–162). San Francisco, CA: Jossey-Bass.

City, E. A., Elmore, R. F., Fiarman, S. E., & Teitel, L. (2009). *Instructional rounds in education: A network approach to improving teaching and learning*. Cambridge, MA: Harvard Education Press.

Coburn, C.E. (2006). Framing the problem of reading instruction: Using frame analysis to uncover the micro-processes of policy implementation. *American Educational Research Journal, 43*(3), 343–379.

Cohen, D. K. (2011). *Teaching and its predicaments*. Cambridge, MA: Harvard University Press.

Cohen, D. K., & Moffitt, S. L. (2009). *The ordeal of equality: Did federal regulation fix the schools?* Cambridge, MA: Harvard University Press.

Common Core State Standards Initiative. (2017). *Appendix B: Text exemplars and sample performance tasks. English language arts & literacy in history/social studies, science, and technical subjects*. Retrived from www.corestandards.org/

Covey, S. (1989). *The 7 habits of effective people*. New York, NY: Simon & Schuster.

Delpit. L. (2006). *Other people's children: Cultural conflict in the classroom* (2nd ed.). New York, NY: W. W. Norton.

Dewey, J. (1990). *The school and society; And the child and the curriculum*. Chicago, IL: University of Chicago Press. (Originally published 1899.)

Doyle, W. (1983). Academic work. *Review of Educational Research, 53*(2), 159–199.

Duckor, B., & Holmberg, C. (2017). *Mastering formative assessment moves: 7 high-leverage practices to advance student learning*. Alexandria, VA: ASCD.

Duckworth, A. (2016). *Grit: The power of passion and perseverance*. New York, NY: Scribner.

DuFour, R. (2016). *In praise of American educators: And how they can become better*. Bloomington, IN: Solution Tree.

DuFour, R., Eaker, R. & DuFour, R. (Eds.). (2005). *On common ground*. Bloomington, IN: Solution Tree.

Duncan, G. J., & Murnane, R. J. (2011). *Whither opportunity? Rising inequality, schools, and children's life chances*. New York, NY: Russell Sage Foundation and the Spencer Foundation.

Duncan, G. J., & Murnane, R. J. (2014). *Restoring opportunity: The crisis of inequality and the challenge for American education.* Cambridge, MA: Harvard Education Press/New York, NY: Russell Sage Foundation.

Dweck, C. S. (2006). *Mindset: The new psychology of success.* New York, NY: Ballantine.

Edwards, C., Gandini, L., & Forman, G. (Eds.). (2012). *The hundred languages of children: The Reggio Emilia experience in transformation.* Santa Barbara, CA: Praeger.

Elmore, R. F. (2008). *Improving the instructional core.* (Unpublished manuscript) Harvard University Graduate School of Education. Retrieved from www.educationallysavvy.com/wp-content/uploads/2016/12/Improving-the-Instructional-Core.pdf

Emdin, C. (2016). *For white folks who teach in the hood, and the rest of y'all too.* Boston, MA: Beacon.

Erdrich, L. (1999). *The Birchbark House.* New York, NY: Hyperion.

Ericsson, A., & Pool, R. (2016). *Peak: Secrets from the new science of expertise.* Boston, MA: Houghton Mifflin Harcourt.

Feiman-Nemser, S. (2012). *Teachers as learners.* Cambridge, MA: Harvard Education Press.

Fischer, F. (2003). *Reframing public policy: Discursive politics and deliberative practices.* New York, NY: Oxford University Press.

Fisher, J. (2016, August 11). Schools that accept "no excuses" from students are not helping them. *Washington Post.* Retrieved from www.washingtonpost.com/posteverything/wp/2016/08/11/schools-that-accept-no-excuses-from-students-are-not-helping-them/?utm_term=.7adcfea88ef0/

Fountas, I.C., & Pinnell, G. S. (2016). *Guided reading: Responsive teaching across the grades* (2nd ed.). Portsmouth, NH: Heinemann.

Frankovich, J., Longhurst, C. A., & Sutherland, S. M. (2011). Evidence-based medicine in the EMR era. *New England Journal of Medicine, 365*(19), 1758–1759.

Fullan, M. (2016). *The new meaning of educational change* (5th ed.). New York, NY: Teachers College Press.

Gandini, L., Hill, L., Cadwell, L., & Schwall, C. (2015). *In the spirit of the studio: Learning from the* atelier *of Reggio Emilia* (2nd ed.). New York, NY: Teachers College Press.

Gawande, A. (2009). *The checklist manifesto.* New York, NY: Henry Holt.

Gay, G. (2010). *Culturally responsive teaching: Theory, research, and practice.* New York, NY: Teachers College Press.

Goffman, E. (1974). *Frame analysis.* Cambridge, MA: Harvard University Press.

Gold, T., Lent, J., Cole, R., Kemple, J., Nathanson, L., & Brand, J. (2012). *Usage patterns and perceptions of the achievement reporting and innovation system (ARIS).* New York, NY: Research Alliance for New York City Schools, New York University.

Goodlad, J. I. (1984). *A place called school.* New York, NY: McGraw-Hill.

Greeley, K. (2000). *Why fly that way? Linking community and academic achievement*. New York, NY: Teachers College Press.

Green, E. (2015). *Building a better teacher: How teaching works*. New York, NY: W. W. Norton.

Harris, E.A. (2016, September 21). Cuomo called for "reboot" of school standards. Officials propose tweaks instead. *New York Times*.

Hawkins, D. (1974). I, thou, it. In D. Hawkins (Ed.), *The informed vision: Essays on learning and human nature* (pp. 49–62). New York, NY: Agathon Books,

Herold, B. (2014, May 2). InBloom's collapse shines spotlight on data-sharing challenges. *Education Week*. Retrieved from www.edweek.org/ew/articles/2014/05/02/30inbloom.h33.html/

Herold, B. (2016a, January 11). The future of big data and analytics in K–12 education. *Education Week*. Retrieved from www.edweek.org/ew/articles/2016/01/13/the-future-of-big-data-and-analytics.html

Herold, B. (2016b, October 21). "Big data" research effort faces student-privacy questions. *Education Week*. Retrieved from www.edweek.org/ew/articles/2014/10/22/09learnsphere.h34.html/

Herold, B., & Doran, L. (2016, January 6). U.S. ed-tech plan calls attention to "digital-use divide." *Education Week*. Retrieved from www.edweek.org/ew/articles/2016/01/06/us-ed-tech-plan-calls-attention-to-digital-use.html/

High Tech High. (2018). *HTH student projects*. Retrieved from www.hightechhigh.org/student-work/student-projects/

Himmele, P., & Himmele, W. (2011). *Total participation techniques*. Alexandria, VA: ASCD.

Ho, A. (2017). *Advancing educational research and student privacy in the "big data" era*. Washington, DC: National Academy of Education.

Horn, I. (2010). Teaching replays, teaching rehearsals, and re-visions of practice: Learning from colleagues in a mathematics teacher community. *Teachers College Record, 112*(1), 225–259.

Isacoff, N.M., Karin, D., & McDonald, J. P. (2018). Adjustment in practice: A critical response to data-driven instruction. In N. Barnes and H. Fives (Eds.), *Cases of teachers' data use* (pp. 162–175). New York, NY: Routledge.

Jackson, P. W. (1968). *Life in classrooms*. New York, NY: Holt, Rinehart & Winston.

James, T. (2000). *Kurt Hahn and the aims of education*. Retrieved from www.outwardbound.fi/tiedostot/Kirjallisuus/Biography.pdf

Jensen, E. (2009). *Teaching with poverty in mind: What being poor does to kids' brains, and what schools can do about it*. Alexandria, VA: ASCD.

Kirkland, D. E. (2013). *A search past silence: The literacy of young black men*. New York, NY: Teachers College Press.

Kobrin, D. (1992). *In there with the kids*. Boston, MA: Houghton-Mifflin.

Koretz, D. (2008). *Measuring up: What educational testing really tells us*. Cambridge, MA: Harvard University Press.

Krechevsky, M., Mardell, B., Rivard, M., & Wilson, D. (2013). *Visible learners: Promoting Reggio-inspired approaches in all schools*. San Francisco, CA: Jossey-Bass.

Ladson-Billings, G. (2009). *The dreamkeepers: Successful teachers of African-American children* (2nd ed.). San Francisco, CA: Jossey-Bass.

Lampert, M. (1985). How do teachers manage to teach? Perspectives on problems of practice. *Harvard Educational Review, 55*(2), 178–194. Retrieved from www-personal.umich.edu/~mlampert/lampert%20pdfs/Lampert_1985.pdf

Lampert, M. (2001). *Teaching problems and the problems of teaching*. New Haven, CT: Yale University Press.

Lampert, M., & Ball, D. L. (1998). *Teaching, multimedia, and mathematics: Investigations of real practice*. New York, NY: Teachers College Press.

Lawrence-Lightfoot, S. (2000). *Respect: An exploration*. Cambridge, MA: Perseus Books.

Lawrence-Lightfoot, S. & Davis, J. H. (1997). *The art and science of portraiture*. San Francisco, CA: Jossey-Bass.

Lee, C. D. (2007). *Culture, literacy, and learning: Taking bloom in the midst of the whirlwind*. New York, NY: Teachers College Press.

Lemov, D. (2015). *Teach like a champion, 2.0*. San Francisco, CA: Jossey-Bass.

Lemov, D., Driggs, C., & Woolway, E. (2016). *Reading reconsidered: A practical guide to literacy instruction*. San Francisco, CA: Jossey-Bass.

Little, J. W. (1982). Norms of collegiality and experimentation: Work place conditions of school success. *American Educational Research Journal, 19*, 325–340.

Little, J. W. (2012). Understanding data use practice among teachers: The contribution of micro-process studies. *American Journal of Education, 18*(2), 143–166.

Lortie, D. C. (1975). *Schoolteacher: A sociological study*. Chicago, IL: University of Chicago Press.

Marshall, R., & Tucker, M. (1992). *Thinking for a living: Education and the wealth of nations*. New York, NY: Basic Books.

Marzano, R. J. (2006). *Classroom assessment and grading that work*. Alexandria, VA: ASCD.

Marzano, R. J. (2007). *The art and science of teaching: A comprehensive framework for effective instruction*. Alexandria, VA: ASCD.

McBride, L., Bailey, A., & Lautzenheiser, D. (2015). *How to help teachers get better together*. Boston, MA: Boston Consulting Group. Retrieved from image-src.bcg.com/Images/BCG-How-to-Help-Teachers-Nov-2015_tcm9-59880.pdf

McDonald, J. P. (1992). *Teaching: Making sense of an uncertain craft*. New York, NY: Teachers College Press.

McDonald, J. P. (2014). *American school reform: What works, what fails, and why*. Chicago, IL: University of Chicago Press.

McDonald, J. P., Fraser, J. W., & Neuman, S. B. (2016). *Where is the Common Core headed? To oblivion, probably*. New York, NY: Education Solutions Initiative, NYU Steinhardt. Retrieved from www.steinhardt.nyu.edu/e/i2/edsolutions/201609/3CommonCore.pdf

McDonald, J. P., Klein, E. J., & Riordan, M. (2009). *Going to scale with new school designs: Reinventing high school.* New York, NY: Teachers College Press.

McDonald, J. P., Mohr, N., Dichter, A., & McDonald, E. C. (2013). *The power of protocols: An educator's guide to better practice* (3rd. ed.). New York, NY: Teachers College Press.

McLaughlin, M. W. (1974). *Evaluation and reform: The Elementary and Secondary Education Act of 1965, Title I.* Santa Monica, CA: The Rand Corporation. Retrieved from www.rand.org/content/dam/rand/pubs/reports/2009/R1292.pdf

McLaughlin, M. W. (1987). Learning from experience: Lessons from policy implementation. *Educational Evaluation and Policy Analysis, 9*(2), 171–178.

McLaughlin, M. W., & Talbert, J. E. (2006). *Building school-based teacher learning communities: Professional strategies to improve student achievement.* New York, NY: Teachers College Press.

Merseth, K. K., with Cooper, K., Roberts, J., Tieken, M.C., Valent, J., & Wynne, C. (2009). *Inside urban charter schools.* Cambridge, MA: Harvard Education Press.

Montgomery, S., & Bishop, N. (2004). *The tarantula scientist.* New York, NY: Houghton Mifflin Harcourt.

National Academy of Education. (2017). *Big data in education: Balancing the benefits of educational research and student privacy: Workshop summary.* Washington, DC: National Academy of Education.

National Research Council. (2001). *How people learn: Brain, mind, experience, and school* (expanded ed.). Washington, DC: National Academies Press.

Neuman, S. B. (2016). Code red: The danger of data-driven instruction. *Educational Leadership, 74*(3), November, 24–29.

Newmann, F. M., & Wehlage, G. G. (1995). *Successful school restructuring.* Madison, WI: Center on Organization and Restructuring of Schools, University of Wisconsin.

New York City Community Health Profiles. (2015). *Profiles by borough.* Retrieved from www1.nyc.gov/site/doh/data/data-publications/profiles.page/

New York City Department of Education. (2015). Online reports. Retrieved from http://schools.nyc.gov/accountability/tools/report/default.htm

Nieto, S. (2010). *The light in their eyes: Creating multi-cultural learning communities* (10th anniversary ed.). New York, NY: Teachers College Press.

Noguera, P. (2003). *City schools and the American dream: Re-claiming the promise of public education.* New York, NY: Teachers College Press.

Nonaka, I. (2007, July–August). The knowledge-creating company. *Harvard Business Review.* Retrieved from www.hbr.org/2007/07/the-knowledge-creating-company/ (Original publication 1991)

Novak, S. (2014). *Student-led discussions: How do I promote rich conversations about books, videos, and other media?* Alexandria, VA: ASCD.

Oakes, J., & Lipton, M. (2002). *Teaching to change the world.* New York, NY: McGraw-Hill.

O' Day, J. A., Bitter, C. S., & Gomez, L. (Eds.). (2011). *Education reform in New York City: Ambitious change in the nation's most complex school system.*

Cambridge, MA: Harvard Education Press.

Oppenheimer, T. (1999, September). Schooling the imagination. *The Atlantic*. Retrieved from www.theatlantic.com/magazine/archive/1999/09/schooling-imagination/309180/

Paterson, K. (1991). *Lyddie*. New York, NY: Puffin Books.

Panero, N. S., & Talbert, J. E. (2013). *Strategic inquiry: Starting small for big results in education*. Cambridge, MA: Harvard Education Press.

Philbrick, R. (1993). *Freak the mighty*. New York, NY: Scholastic.

Popham, W. J. (2003). The seductive allure of data, *Educational Leadership, 60*(5), 48–51.

Powell, A. G., Farrar, E., & Cohen, D. K. (1985). *The shopping mall high school: Winners and losers in the educational marketplace*. Boston, MA: Houghton-Mifflin.

Price, J., & Koretz, D. (2013). Building assessment literacy. In K. P. Boudett, E. A. City, & R. J. Murnane (Eds.). *Data wise: A step-by-step guide to using assessment results to improve teaching and learning* (Revised and expanded ed., pp. 35–66). Cambridge, MA: Harvard Education Press.

Reeves, A. R. (2011). *Where great teaching begins: Planning for student thinking and learning*. Alexandria, VA: ASCD.

Resnick, L. B., & Wirt, J. (Eds.). (1996). *Linking school and work: Roles for standards and assessment*. San Francisco, CA: Jossey-Bass.

Rhodes, J. (2012). *An education in politics: The origins and evolution of no child left behind*. Ithaca, NY: Cornell University Press.

Richert, A. E. (2012). *What should I do? Confronting dilemmas of teaching in urban schools*. New York, NY: Teachers College Press.

Riessman, C. K. (2008). *Narrative methods for the human sciences*. Thousand Oaks, CA: SAGE.

Ritchart, R., Church, M., & Morrison, K. (2011). *Making thinking visible*. San Francisco, CA: Jossey-Bass.

Scholastic & Bill and Melinda Gates Foundation. (2012). *Primary sources: 2012: America's teachers on the teaching profession*. New York, NY: Scholastic. Retrieved from www.scholastic.com/primarysources/pdfs/Gates2012_full.pdf

Schön, D. A. (1983). *The reflective practitioner: How professionals think in action*. New York, NY: Basic Books.

Schön, D. A., & Rein, M. (1994). *Frame reflection: Toward the resolution of intractable policy controversies*. New York, NY: Basic Books.

Sedlak, M. W., Wheeler, C. W., Pullin, D. C., & Cusick, P. A. (1986). *Selling students short: Classroom bargains and academic reform in the American high school*. New York, NY: Teachers College Press.

Seidenberg, M. (2017). *Language at the speed of sight: How we read, why so many can't, and what can be done about it*. New York, NY: Basic Books.

Shulman, L. (1987). Knowledge and teaching: Foundations of the new reform. *Harvard Educational Review, 57*, 1–22.

Siman, N., Goldenberg, S. M., & Gold, T. (2014). *Digital collaboration and classroom practice: Educator use of ARIS Connect*. New York, NY: Research Alliance for New York City Schools, New York University.

Singleton, G. E. (2015). *Courageous conversations about race: A fieldguide for achieving equity in schools*. Thousand Oaks, CA: Corwin.

Sizer, T. R. (1984). *Horace's compromise: The dilemma of the American high school*. Boston, MA: Houghton-Mifflin.

Sizer, T. R. (2013). *The new American high school*. San Francisco, CA: Jossey-Bass.

Sizer, T. R., & Sizer N. F. (1999). *The students are watching: Schools and the moral contract*. Boston, MA: Beacon Press.

Snow, D. A., & Benford, R. D. (1992). Master frames and cycles of protest. In A. D. Morris & C. M. Mueller (Eds.), *Frontiers in social movement theory* (pp. 133–155). New Haven, CT: Yale University Press.

Sparks, S. D. (2016, January 7). Highlighting NCLB-era research. *Education Week*. Retrieved from www.edweek.org/ew/articles/2016/01/07/highlightingno-child-left-behind-act-era-research.html/

Spencer Foundation. (2012). *Request for research proposals: Evidence for the Classroom: Investigating whether, when, and how student performance data inform instruction*. Chicago, IL: Author.

Spillane, J. P. (2006). *Distributed leadership*. San Francisco, CA: Jossey-Bass.

Spillane, J. P. (2012). Data in practice: Conceptualizing the data-based decision-making phenomena. *American Journal of Education, 118*(2), 113–141.

Spillane, J. P. (2014, February 7). *Untitled talk at the Spencer Foundation Data Project meeting*. Chicago, Illinois.

Spillane, J. P., & Diamond, J. B. (2007). (Eds.) *Distributed leadership in practice*. New York, NY: Teachers College Press.

Spillane, J. P., Parise, L. M., & Sherer, J. Z. (2011). Organizational routines as coupling mechanisms: Policy, school administration, and the technical core. *American Educational Research Journal, 48*(3), 586–619.

Standen, A. (2014, September 29). *How big data is changing medicine*. Retrieved from ww2.kqed.org/science/2014/09/29/how-big-data-is-changing-medicine/

Sutcher, L., Darling-Hammond, L., & Carver-Thomas, D. (2016, September 15). A coming crisis in teaching? Teacher supply, demand, and shortages in the U.S. *Learning Policy Institute*. Retrieved from www.learningpolicyinstitute.org/product/coming-crisis-teaching/

Taylor, K. (2016, February 12). At Success Academy School, a stumble in math and a teacher's anger on video. *New York Times*.

TCRWP. (2017). Our history. *Teachers College Reading and Writing Project, Columbia University*. Retrieved from www.readingandwritingproject.org/about/history/

Tough, P. (2012). *How children succeed: Grit, curiosity, and the hidden power of character*. Boston, MA: Houghton Mifflin Harcourt.

Tough, P. (2016). *Helping children succeed: What works and why*. Boston, MA: Houghton Mifflin Harcourt.

Tyack, D. B. (1974). *The one best system: A history of American urban education*. Cambridge, MA: Harvard University Press.

U.S. Congress. (1965). *Senate Subcommittee on Education: Hearings on Elementary and Secondary Education Act of 1965* (89th Congress, 1st session). Washington, DC: GPO.

Waller, W. (1932). *The sociology of teaching.* New York, NY: Russell & Russell.

Weick, K. E. (1976). Educational organizations as loosely coupled systems. *Administrative Science Quarterly, 21*(1), 1–19.

Wenger, E., McDermott, R., & Snyder, W. M. (2002). *Cultivating communities of practice: A guide to managing knowledge.* Boston, MA: Harvard Business School Press.

Wilson, W. J. (2012). *Truly disadvantaged: The inner city, the underclass, and public policy* (2nd ed.). Chicago, IL: University of Chicago Press.

Wormeli, R. (2006). *Fair isn't always equal: Assessing and grading in the differentiated classroom.* Portland, ME: Stenhouse Publishers.

Zwiers, J. (2014). *Building academic language.* San Francisco, CA: Jossey-Bass.

Index

About the Authors

Joseph P. McDonald led the research team and is the author or coauthor of 10 books about schooling and teaching. They include the bestselling *Power of Protocols* as well as the PROSE Award winner for 2015, *American School Reform: What Works, What Fails, and Why*. He is emeritus professor in the Department of Teaching and Learning at the Steinhardt School, New York University, and a former English teacher.

Nora M. Isacoff joined the research team as a postdoctoral research scientist in the Department of Teaching and Learning at New York University. She holds a PhD in cognitive psychology from Rutgers University. Her work as both researcher and practitioner applies basic psychological principles to complex problems of learning. She currently works in private practice as a learning specialist.

Dana Karin joined the research team as a PhD candidate in Teaching and Learning at New York University. Her research interests include teacher retention in public schools. A graduate of Brown University, Dana taught middle and high school social studies and Spanish in Connecticut, Rhode Island, and Colorado. She was a founding teacher at The Peak School, a progressive middle and high school in the Rocky Mountains.